To Kathy and [illegible] one
Best wishes – [illegible]
Francis A. Lord
December 1966

of.
Signed

Bands and Drummer Boys of the Civil War

BANDS AND DRUMMER

THOMAS YOSELOFF

NEW YORK · SOUTH BRUNSWICK · LONDON

BOYS OF THE CIVIL WAR

Francis A. Lord and Arthur Wise

Thomas Yoseloff, *Publisher*
South Brunswick, New Jersey

Thomas Yoseloff Ltd
18 Charing Cross Road
London W.C. 2, England

6408
Printed in the United States of America

Acknowledgements

Robert and Adrian Miller, Falls Church, Va. Dr. Robert S. Chamberlain, Alexandria, Va. Paul Nachtrab, II, Colorado Springs, Colo. Roy Smith, Chicago, Ill.

To the following authors and publishers: Holt, Rinehart and Winston, Inc., for permission to quote from Burke Divis' *Our Incredible Civil War;* Harper and Row, Publishers, for permission to quote from Margaret Leech's *Reveille in Washington;* Bobbs-Merrill Company, Inc., for permission to quote from *The Life of Billy Yank,* by Bell Irvin Wiley, copyright 1952, 1962; University of California Press, for permission to quote from Abner Small's *The Road to Richmond;* Appleton-Century Book Publishers, for permission to quote from James H. Wilson's *Under the Old Flag;* and Harry H. Hall, author, and the North Carolina Confederate Centennial Commission, publishers of *A Johnny Reb.*

Foreword

An army is the reflection of a people and military music is a reflection of the army. Certainly the animated "Marseillaise" reflected the spirit of 1792 France. In the Civil War, Southern impetuosity found its best musical expression in the stirring strains of "Dixie," while the North's inexorable will to preserve the Union was splendidly expressed in the measured beat of the "Battle Hymn of the Republic."

Up to 1861 it was a popular notion that armies marched to battle inspired by the patriotic strains of bands, and the martial airs of fife and drum. Generally speaking, this was not the case during the Civil War. Musicians of all types certainly were found on the battlefield, but with the exception of buglers, the musicians were usually seen carrying off wounded on stretchers or assisting surgeons at field hospitals, rather than playing military music.

Behind the front lines, military bands were stationed at the large base hospitals and recruiting depots. The sick and wounded in hospitals were invigorated by the airs they had come to love. Many who had the "blues" or were in the first stages of disease, were revived and strengthened.

In time of war the music of a band, when carefully selected and well performed, is an important aid in keeping up the discipline and soldierly bearing of the men. It is true that musicians generally did not go into battle and charge the enemy's strong positions with a flourish of trumpets and clashing of cymbals. Yet the precision of a good military band was of inestimable value for the newly-forming regiments.

For the sick and wounded the band brought memories of home and other cherished associations. As one veteran put it: "Don't forget to put in the book how we boys used to yell at the band for music to cheer us up when we were tramping along so tired that we could hardly drag one foot after the other. That good old tune . . . 'Hell on the Rappahannock' had enough music in it to make a man who was just about dead brace up, throw his chest out and take the step as if he had received a new lease on life."

Music played an important part for the Civil War volunteer from the very moment he thought of enlisting. Patriotic mass meetings were held in every town, village and hamlet. The entire population, male and female, old and young, flocked to these meetings to hear speeches and listen to martial music. Drums and fifes were everywhere. Often the flag was suspended over a large bass drum on which the eager volunteers signed the enlistment rolls.

While the number of Confederate bands was limited, about every Federal regiment which went to the front in 1861 and 1862 had its own brass band and many also had fife and drum corps. In late 1862 the regimental brass bands were mustered out of service and their place taken by brigade bands. This was an economy move but its effect on morale was adverse. For example, when Gilmore's Band, attached to the 24th Massachusetts Infantry, was discharged August 1862, the regimental commander wrote: "I think it a great mistake and that the service will lose more than the treasury will gain."

This is the story of *Military* bands. References to bands on board ships are few. And when such instances are encountered the references are almost invariably to organizational units of the army, en route to the front, especially to enemy-held ports and coastal defences on the Atlantic coastline. Such was the situation when Fort Walker, a defensive bastion on the South Carolina coast, fell into Federal hands in November 1861. As the United States flag was run up above the captured fort, the bands on the Federal vessels in the harbor broke out with the "Star Spangled Banner."

SOURCES

In the preparation of this work, many official and non-official sources have been utilized. The National Archives contains much material on bands and bandsmen. Over four hundred regimental histories were studied but with rather surprising results. Due to the veterans' tendency to regard their bandsmen as unimportant non-combatants, most regimental historians relegated the band to an insignificant role. Often the bandsmen were only listed in the roster at the end of the volume. But occasionally (especially if a bandsman was on the pub-

lication committee), the band received its just due.

In addition to personal reminiscences of Civil War musicians, the author has utilized manuscript letters written by bandsmen at the front. Some material has been found in general histories and biographical studies of the War. While the Official Records of the Union and Confederate armies and navies yielded little, the Regulations and various contemporary manuals were most helpful. A bibliography of all books actually cited will be found at the end of the book. However, it should be emphasized that this bibliography only faintly reflects the very extensive source material examined in preparing this book. Unfortunately, much of the source material contained little or nothing on bands of the 1861-1865 period. This book is an attempt to fill many of the gaps which heretofore have existed with relation to the role of bands in the War. That role was indeed an important one!

The author's collection of Civil War letters includes a group of original letters written to and by Musician Roland F. Barrows, Regimental band, 18th Massachusetts Infantry. These letters written in 1861-1862, numbering 22 in all, are lengthy and, while not including spectacular revelations of Civil War bandsmen, are valuable in giving contemporary "color" and authenticity to this book.

Much material is available in the National Archives under the heading "Records Relating to Army Bands." This material from the office of the adjutant general consists of a box of materials relating to army bands, individual members of bands, and band masters. The material is arranged alphabetically by initial letter of surname of person.

The *Confederate Veteran* a magazine published for over forty years, received many contributions from men who either served in or appreciated the band music of the

Confederate Army. Mr. Roy Smith of Chicago, Illinois, has been very helpful in locating material on bands in the *Confederate Veteran*. The results of his thorough research are to be seen throughout this book.

Contents

Bands and Drummer Boys of the Civil War

BEAT! BEAT! DRUMS!
Beat! Beat! Drums! Blow! Bugles! Blow.
Through the windows—through doors—
    burst like a ruthless force,
Into the solemn church, and scatter the
    congregation;
Into the school where the scholar is studying;

. . .

Let not the child's voice be heard, nor
    the mother's entreaties;
Make even the trestles to shake the dead,
    where they lie awaiting the hearses,
So strong you thump, O terrible drums—
So loud you bugles blow.
        — *Drum Taps*, Walt Whitman

1. American Military and Civilian Bands 1775-1860

American bands of the 1775-1860 period inherited a long tradition of band music and musicians, dating back at least to the ancient Egyptians. It is known that Egyptians paraded to the accompaniment of reed pipes, tambourines, and trumpets. Not only the Assyrians but also the Hebrews, Romans, Greeks and other early peoples had their band music. Certainly, one of the most famous parades of all time was the march around Jericho with the blowing of rams' horns. The Romans had the tuba, the cornet, and cavalry trumpets. As early as 570 B.C. bronze trumpets were used in the Roman legions. Most ancient peoples used drums of various kinds. By the 18th century, military music had become fairly well standardized. Frequent allusions are made in French works of the 18th century to the superiority of German music. It has maintained this superiority to the present day. However, some excellent French and British bands trace their heritage back to the latter part of the 18th century and the early years of the 19th, and it is from the traditional French and British military marches and tunes that much of American military music descended, or was in fact, actually copied.

Band music in America initially made slow progress. Fifes and drums were the only musical instruments used by our troops during the Revolutionary War. It was not until 1798 that an act of Congress authorized a Marine band, to consist of a drum major, a fife major and 32 drums and fifes. On August 21, 1800, the Marine Band gave a concert in Washington. The Marine Band is the oldest American military band and was the only band in Washington until the 1830's. Since Jefferson's day this band has played at every inauguration when that ceremony called for the presence of a band. During the Civil War it was a potent morale-booster, Lincoln insisted that it continue its outdoor concerts and frequently called upon it to play at the White House. It was present when Lincoln spoke at Gettysburg in November 1863.

At the outbreak of war in 1861, brass bands had become very popular in the United States. These bands ranged in size from ten to thirty pieces. The only Federal band to stay together throughout the war was the band of the 114th Pennsylvania Infantry (Collis' Zouaves). Other famous bands were the Stonewall Brigade Band of Staunton, Virginia; the Fencible Band of

Home made cigar fiddle. (From the Frick Art Reference Library of New York City)

Lull in the fight. (From the Frick Art Reference Library of New York City, Union League Club, by Edwin Forbes)

Lancaster, Pennsylvania; the 26th North Carolina Regiment Band (Moravians); and such popular civilian bands as Gilmore's and Dodsworth's. However, there were many others. Philadelphia provided at least twenty such bands. In New York City, the 115th Regiment had a band as early as 1810, and by 1823 there were five bands in the city. Several Negro bands competed—often successfully—for the musical business in New York.

Noll's 7th New York Infantry Band lost popularity with the regiment because of an incident* which occurred during an excursion to Richmond in 1858. The contract with Noll expired in November of that year and in December C. S. Grafulla was engaged as bandmaster. He was highly recommended as "a capable leader and composer, who had for twenty years been identified with the

military music of the city and country." The new band-master was authorized to select 38 musicians for the new band, and a contract was made for new uniforms and equipments.

Early in February 1860, the new 7th Regiment Band made its first public appearance. On February 18th it gave a concert at the Academy of Music, assisted by several eminent vocalists. Although the day and evening were very stormy, the house was crowded and the concert was a success. From this time on, the band went to local and national celebrations and by April 1861 had a well-deserved reputation as being one of the leading bands in the country.

This band led the 7th down Broadway in April 1861, its music almost drowned out by the cheering of thousands of semi-hysterical onlookers. Later in the war, when Admiral Lesoffsky and the officers of the Russian fleet were officially received by the Mayor and Common Council of New York City, the band paraded with 37 members in line.

One of the famous bands of the late 1850's was the "Fencible Band" of Lancaster, Pennsylvania. This band, organized in 1856, participated in the inaugural parade of

* The trouble in Richmond was due to the "mutinous conduct" of Noll and his musicians. The fatigue of the journey, the heat of the weather, and perhaps the free flow of wine and lager-beer had demoralized the band, and Noll, who was a poor disciplinarian, could not control his men, even if he was so inclined. The band was reluctant to parade in Richmond and throughout the trip was distinguished for its "indifference, sullenness and constant grumbling." Apparently Noll did not realize that hot weather and lots of beer do not combine to make precise marching or good music!

Drummer boy. (From the Cooper Union Museum of New York City)

President Buchanan, as well as various other public events. It went to the front with the 1st Pennsylavnia Infantry in April 1861. On the return of that unit, the band became a part of the 79th Pennsylvania Infantry. It later became a brigade band, which indicates very clearly its over-all proficiency, since those regimental bands selected to continue in service were very generally superior to the other regimental bands of their brigade.

The York, Pennsylvania, Band, composed of 30 men, was organized some time prior to 1838. During that year it participated in a July 4th celebration in Harrisburg, at which time it was highly praised for the excellent quality of its music.

The Spring Garden Band, organized in East York, Pennsylvania, prior to 1861, entered the service at the outbreak of hostilities as the regimental band for the 87th Pennsylvania Infantry. It continued in the

Bugler boys. (From the Cooper Union Museum of New York City)

**Bugler on Horseback, "Bugle Call" in action.
(Charcoal sketch from the Library of Congress,
painted in 1863 by W.M. Hunt, and used on the
frontpiece of Volume I of Battles and Leaders of
the Civil War)**

service for two years and as late as 1907 was still active. When the 87th marched to Towsontown, Maryland, on May 30, 1862, the band, under Captain Wm. Frey, played patriotic selections beginning and concluding with "The Star Spangled Banner."

In the fall of 1859, some 20 young men of Manchester, New Hampshire, formed a class for the study of band music, and employed Edwin T. Baldwin as instructor. In the summer of 1860, they organized "Baldwin's Cornet Band" and were employed that year by the Republican committee to furnish music at parades and political meetings during the presidential campaign. This band accompanied the 1st New Hampshire Infantry to the front in 1861. Most of the members were excellent singers, and as vocalists they added greatly to the entertainment of the regiment.

Gilmore's Band was formed by Patrick S. Gilmore, who was born in Ireland, and who succeeded in overcoming his parents' plan of making him a priest by turning instead to a career of music. His childhood was spent in a garrison town and young Gilmore spent all his spare hours with the regimental bands. A band leader took him in hand and put him through such a course of harmony and instrumentation that in a short time he could play any instrument in the local amateur band and for which he composed several musical pieces.

Gilmore came to Boston shortly before the Civil War and in a few years had organized the band bearing his own name, with which he soon won a national reputation.

In 1861 he was selected by the 24th Massachusetts Infantry to head their band. Nothing contributed more to the early prestige of that regiment than the fact that its officers were able to take with them in their army life the most famous musical aggregation at that time in the country. The band was easily the star wherever military music was

in question, and the strains of excellent music which accompanied the progress of the regiment southward captivated all listeners. Whether delighting Governor Hicks and his associates in Annapolis, or entertaining General Burnside and staff in Newbern, Gilmore and his men always played their best and "there could be no better." When Arbuckle placed the cornet to his lips and played "The Last Rose of Summer" or "Annie Laurie" there was nothing doing within the sound of his notes but listening. Need anyone wonder that the Confederate prisoners at Roanoke fairly went wild when, as they were filing down to the transports that were to take them to their homeland, Gilmore and his men struck up "Dixie?" What did it matter that the leader was called down by some higher-up for his act; he had the pleasure of knowing that he had given the enemy one precious moment never to be forgotten.

As nearly perfect as the musicians were in their playing, they could produce discords, as when their application for a furlough was disapproved. Then on their way across the parade ground, there came from the horn instruments some notes which no one believed them capable of blowing! Eventually harmony was restored and the band performed superbly until their muster out of service in late 1862. Gilmore did not forget his old friends in the 24th and very soon after reaching Boston the band gave a concert which netted a good sum for the equipping of a band to be drawn from the enlisted men of the regiment.

Gilmore took the field once again, this time as director of all the bands in the Department of the Gulf. It was in New Orleans, March 4, 1864, that he carried out the first of his famous mass jubilees. The occasion was the inauguration of Michael Hahn as the first Federal Governor of Louisiana. In a city only a year or two out of enemy dominance, Gilmore organized a chorus of 10,000

Discharge papers of Jacob Snyder, a second class musician of the Twenty-sixth Regiment band of Illinois.

CERTIFICATE

TO BE GIVEN TO VOLUNTEERS AT THE TIME OF THEIR DISCHARGE TO ENABLE THEM
TO RECEIVE THEIR PAY, &c.

I CERTIFY, on honor, that *Jacob H Snyder* a *2nd* class *musician* of the
~~of Captain~~ *Band* ~~Company~~ ( ) of the *26th* Regiment of *Infantry*
Volunteers, of the State of *Illinois* , born in *Lancaster* , State
of ~~New York~~ *Ohio* ~~&c~~ , aged *22* years; *5* feet *8* inches high; ~~dark~~ complexion, *dark* eyes
Black hair, and by occupation a ~~farmer~~ *Student* having joined the ~~company on its original organization~~ *Band*
at *Galesburg Ills* , and enrolled in it at the muster into the service of the United States
at *Hannibal Mo* on the *15th* day of ~~September, 186 , (or was~~
~~mustered in service as a recruit~~ by *October 1861.*
~~on the~~ *day of* ~~186 , to serve in the Regiment)~~ for the term
of *three years* : and having served honestly and faithfully with
~~his Company in~~ *the Band* , to the present date, is now entitled to a discharge by reason
of*

Special field Order No 94 Dated Ha Qts Dept of the Miss

Corinth Miss June 8th 1862 ------------------------

The said *Jacob H Snyder* was last paid by Paymaster
Wthwall to include the *28th* day of *February* 186*2*, and has pay due him
from that time to the present date, ~~and also pay for the use of his horse, (having been mounted during the time,)~~
~~and he is entitled to pay and subsistence for traveling to place of enrolment and whatever other allowances~~
~~are authorized to volunteer soldiers, or militia, discharged. He has received~~ ~~100~~
~~dollars advanced by the United States on account of clothing,~~

~~There is to be stopped from him, on account of the State of~~ ~~or other authorities,~~
~~for clothing, &c., received on entering service,~~ ~~100~~ ~~dollars; also, for expenses of subsistence~~
~~for traveling from place of enrolment to the place of rendezvous, amounting to~~ ~~100~~ ~~dollars,~~
~~and on account of the United States for extra clothing received in kind from~~
~~and for other stoppages, viz:~~

The said Jacob H Snyder is entitled to Clothing pay from the 28th
day of February 1862 to the time of discharge ------------
~~amounting to~~ ~~100~~ ~~dollars;~~
~~and he has been subsisted for traveling to his place of enrolment, up to the~~ ~~180~~
~~He is indebted to~~ ~~100~~ ~~dollars.~~
GIVEN in duplicate, at *Corinth Miss*, this *14th* day of *June* , 186*2*

E A Tucker
Adjt Commanding ~~Company~~ *Band*

Comdg 26th Ills Regt

*State particularly the cause of discharge, and whether the disability existed prior to the date of muster, or was contracted after it.

NOTE.—Two of these certificates, (or duplicates,) are to be given to each volunteer soldier who may be discharged previously to the discharge of his company, that he may at once receive from the Paymaster the pay, &c., due him, and the captain (or other officer commanding the company, will certify to the act of the delivery of the duplicate certificates; on these certificates the Soldier is "entitled to" his discharge, and should also present his discharge to the Paymaster to have the payment endorsed on it. The discharge is to be given back to the Soldier, by the Paymaster; the latter only retaining as his voucher the duplicate certificates.

Scene in camp. The Army of the Potomac after evening parade.

The stag dance. A country square dance complete with a fiddler.

Drummer boy, and fear spread by cannon ball.

City of Cairo, Schottisch by Chas J. Young. (From the Franklin D. Roosevelt Library, Hyde Park, New York)

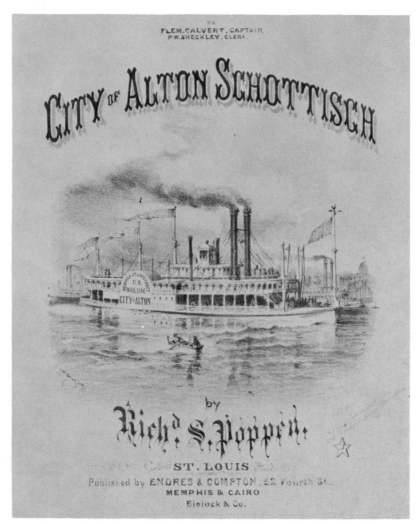

**City of Alton Schottisch, 1864, by R.S. Popper.
(From the Franklin D. Roosevelt Library, Hyde
Park, New York)**

school children, collected an orchestra of
500 players, and, with infantry and artillery
accompaniment, he directed this hetero-
geneous aggregation in patriotic airs, concluding with "The Star Spangled Banner."
In later years Gilmore gave even larger mass
concerts. He believed that if 80 musicians
make good music, 800 must make music ten
times as good. On one occasion, in addition
to a chorus and orchestra of several thousands, Gilmore added a battery of cannon,
half a dozen church bells, and threw in
for good measure 50 firemen in full uniform beating out the "Anvil Chorus" on 50
anvils!

Despite these musical monstrosities, they

did serve to plant the seeds of good music in
hundreds of hamlets where they had not
existed before. Gilmore was a splendid drill-
master. In 1873 he went to New York City
and organized a band for the 22nd New York
National Guard, with which he played in
"Gilmore's Garden." In the 1880's he, along
with young Sousa, Victor Herbert, and
others, drew multitudes. Gilmore and his
band toured Europe several times, where
they were well received. Gilmore also super-
vised the raising of the band for the 2nd
Mass. Inf. whose drum major, Henry Kessel-
huth, had been wounded while serving in the
Brunswick army in 1848. This was an unusual band; of its 24 members, both England

Admiral Farragut's Grand March. (From the Franklin D. Roosevelt Library of Hyde Park, New York)

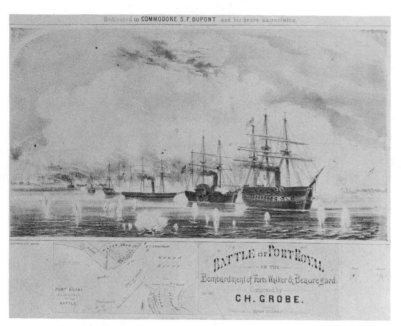

Battle of Port Royal, by C.H. Grobe. (From the Franklin D. Roosevelt Library of Hyde Park, New York)

and Belgium were represented. The band rendered excellent service at Cedar Mountain in removing the wounded from the field, and two of its members were taken prisoner in the process. Several members re-enlisted in the brigade band, after their regimental band was discharged in the fall of 1862. Gilmore died in 1892.

One of the crack Massachusetts militia units in 1861 was the Boston Light Infantry, a battalion of three companies. This battalion of some 250 men was sent to Fort Warren, Boston Harbor, on April 29, 1861. It was known as "The Tigers" and was made up of students and clerks. The Gilmore band was sent to Fort Warren to furnish music for this elite unit.

Civilian bands were occasionally hired for performances at state rendezvous camps. Among the members of a band occasionally engaged for duty on Sundays at Readville, Massachusetts, was Mariani, a former drum major of Gilmore's Band when it was at the zenith of its fame in Boston. Mariani was a

huge physical specimen, jolly and full of anecdotes about his native Italy. "Seignor" Mariani later helped the "Cadet Regiment" (45th Massachusetts Infantry) in its band instruction. When Mariani marched at the head of the band, dressed in his resplendent uniform, with his long gold-headed baton and his bearskin hat, with pompom topping all, he was inspiring. Members of the band of the 45th thought of him as a "moving shield" to cover the defects of their inexperienced work.

These civilian bands were also used to keep up the morale of the home front. One of the bands used extensively for this purpose was Birgfeld's of Philadelphia. This excellent band, which retained its civilian status and never went to the war zone, remained at home, enjoying almost a monopoly of local engagements. It was in great demand for home parades. Shortly before Antietam the band played during the course of a great recruiting drive. Officers were busy writing down the names of volunteers; old and young men, inspired by the

Battle of New Orleans. (From the Franklin D. Roosevelt Library of Hyde Park, New York)

Eagle Quadrille, 1863. (From the Franklin D. Roosevelt Library of Hyde Park, New York)

fervor of the occasion, hurried to the recruiting tents to "sign up." Again, during the month of June 1863, crowds thronged Fairmount Park to enjoy the band's concerts. This band played the "Triumphal March" and "Coronation March" in several victorious celebrations during the war. On July 5, 1863, several military bands paraded through the streets of Philadelphia to celebrate Lee's defeat at Gettysburg. Two days later the Union League in Philadelphia celebrated Meade's victory by marching, with Birgfeld's Band, to Independence Hall.

The 44th Massachusetts Infantry paid three thousand dollars for the services of Flagg's Boston Brass Band, and that for only a brief period. It was not in the contract that such bands should go to war with the regiments with which they had been in camp. On the departure of the troops the bands would escort them to the train or transport and there the duties of the musicians ended.

2. Federal Regimental Bands

The period between the spring of 1861 and mid-summer of 1862—something over a year—was when music was at its best in the army. The militia regiments from the different loyal states went to the front for a three months' tour of duty and each regiment took with it a regimental band, composed generally of the best military professional musicians of the locality from which the regiment took its departure. The short-term troops returned from their tour of duty and were replaced by those of longer terms. Musicians who had served with the three months' troops having gained much in general proficiency and having become familiarized with the military field movements were encouraged to enlist with the long-term regiments that were then being formed. Inducements were held out to quicken the enlistment of recruits by publicly announcing that a famous band would be attached to some particular regiment.

The Federal Army included among its numerous regimental organizations, during the first 18 months of the war, many bands from the Northern, Middle and Western States, which had national reputations as musical organizations. Among these were Gilmore's of Boston, and Grafula's, and Dodsworth's of New York. While the army was stationed near Washington in those early months, visitors to the different camps of the regiments spoke above all else about the excellent band music they heard in the camps. "I heard bands in the Army of the Potomac," said one observer who visited the camps in 1862, "that could play the music of the entire opera in faultless harmony without looking at the notes, from the beginning to the end." While this was doubtless an exaggeration, there were excellent bands in the army at that time, and the rivalry as to which regiment had the best, was nearly as great as the competition in regard to which regiment, brigade, division or corps excelled in the "school of the soldier."

A series of General Orders from the War Department laid down the necessary provisions for the regimental band organization. For the regular army regiments this "charter" was embodied in General Order No. 48, dated July 31, 1861, which provided that bands of the regular regiments would consist of not more than 24 musicians for each regiment of infantry and artillery, and 16 musicians for each regiment of mounted troops.

Each infantry regiment was allowed one drum major or leader of the band, and two principal musicians.

Commodore Winslow's March of grand victory. (From the Franklin D. Roosevelt Library of Hyde Park, New York)

Lincoln Inauguration, 1861. A band was present, probably the U.S. Marine Band.

Each cavalry regiment was allowed two chief buglers.

Each artillery regiment was allowed two principal musicians.

Much more official interest was bestowed on the volunteer regiments. At the beginning of the war every regiment had a full brass band, some numbering as high as 50 pieces. There were from four to five regiments in each brigade, three brigades in each division, three divisions in each corps. This meant that each corps had from between 36-40 bands. Accordingly, it was felt necessary to reduce this number to one band per brigade. Most of the regimental bands actually had 24 members under a "bandmaster." Band leaders took key musicians with them. For example, when William E. Gilmore of Pawtucket, Rhode Island, was selected to be leader of the 25th Massachusetts Infantry band, he took seven men from his home town to be members of the band in their newly adopted state.

As early as October 26, 1861, by General Order No. 91, of the Adjutant General's Office, no more bands for volunteer regiments were to be mustered into service, and no vacancies in existing bands were to be filled. Moreover, all band members who were not musicians were to be discharged by their regimental commanders.

The cost of bands was so heavy that as early as December 5, 1861, the Paymaster General reported that regimental bands were "far more ornamental than useful," and should be abolished. This would result in a saving of about five million dollars.

In December 1861, the United States Sanitary Commission conducted an inspection of the Army of the Potomac. Although sanitation of the camps was of first priority, the Commission was also especially concerned with the soldiers' morale. It discovered that bands were an object of pride to the regiments; out of 200 regiments inspected, 143 had bands, 43 had none, and no reports were available on the remaining 14. Frederick Law Olmsted, Secretary General of

the Commission believed that a military band was indispensable in developing good morale.

As early as January 18, 1862, General McClellan was constrained to issue a general order to his inspectors that, in their tours of inspection, they should inspect the bands of *all* regiments. These inspectors were ordered to discharge all members of the bands who were not musicians.

On June 30, 1862, there were in Federal service about 28,000 men enlisted as musicians of whom about 14,000 were serving as bandsmen in 618 bands. Due to the high cost of these bands, amounting to millions of dollars a year, the War Department ordered the mustering out of service all of regimental bands of volunteers. The General Order 91, (July 29, 1862) which contained the specific orders for the volunteer bands' discharge further stated that all enlisted men who had been detached from companies for the purpose of serving in said bands, but who had not originally been mustered in as

Just after the war, in Baton Rouge, Louisiana. The music has attracted a crowd. Military band, regimental flags, with a candidate for the State Senate making some progress.

The Grand Review, May 23-24, 1865. Two hundred thousand troops marched by in the bright May sunshine. All present but the commander-in-chief.

ALL PRESENT BUT THE COMMANDER-IN-CHIEF

PRESIDENT LINCOLN.—[Photographed by Brady.]

President Lincoln. (A Brady photo)

Grand review, May 23-24, 1865. Two hundred thousand men in blue amid national rejoicing.

Grand review, May 1865. The return of the soldiers with Sherman's troops marching down Pennsylvania Avenue.

One of the proudest days of the nation—May 24, 1865—here lives again. The true greatness of the American people was not displayed till the close of the war. The citizen from the walks of humble life had during the contest become a veteran soldier, equal in courage and fighting capacity to the best drilled infantry of Marlborough, Frederick the Great, or Napoleon. But it remained to be seen whether he would return peacefully to the occupations of peace. European nations made dark predictions. "Would nearly a million men," they asked, "one of the mightiest military organizations ever trained in war, quietly lay aside this restless power and disappear into the unnoted walks of civil life?" Europe with its standing armies thought not. Europe was mistaken. The disbanded veterans lent the effectiveness of military order and discipline to the industrial and commercial development of the land they had come to love with an increased devotion. The pictures are of Sherman's troops marching

THE RETURN OF THE SOLDIERS—THE GRAND REVIEW

down Pennsylvania Avenue. The horsemen in the lead are General Francis P. Blair and his staff, and the infantry in flashing new uniforms are part of the Seventeenth Corps in the Army of Tennessee. Little over a year before, they had started with Sherman on his series of battles and flanking marches in the struggle for Atlanta. They had taken a conspicuous and important part in the battle of July 22d east of Atlanta, receiving and finally repulsing attacks in both front and rear. They had marched with Sherman to the sea and participated in the capture of Savannah. They had joined in the campaign through the Carolinas, part of the time leading the advance and tearing up many miles of railway track, and operating on the extreme right after the battle of Bentonville. After the negotiations for Johnston's surrender were completed in April, they set out on the march for the last time with flying colors and martial music, to enter the memorable review at Washington in May, here preserved

THE SAME SCENE, A FEW SECONDS LATER

Peacemakers, March 1865. (Painted by C.P.A. Healy, printed in the National Geographic Society, and copy lent by the White House)

32

band members, were to return to duty with their line companies. Since these men had not been enlisted as musicians, they were not entitled to discharge as such.

With their own consent, *musicians* of regimental bands, instead of being discharged, could be transferred, on their current enlistment, to form the brigade bands authorized by Section 6 of the General Order, at the discretion of the brigade commanders.

Section 6 provided that each brigade in the volunteer service could have 16 musicians as a band, whose members would receive the pay and allowances already provided by law for the regimental bands, except that the band leader of a brigade band would receive forty-five dollars per month with the emoluments and allowances of a quartermaster sergeant.

REGIMENTAL BANDS IN THE EAST

One of the "show outfits" of Washington was the United States Marine Band. This band was a great morale booster for new regiments arriving from the North. On August 16, 1862, as the 122nd Pennsylvania Infantry wearily moved into temporary barracks in the capital city, about 11 P.M. the Marine Band visited their quarters and paid the Pennsylvanians the compliment of a serenade. This was intended to cheer up the boys but it only kept them from going to bed and getting a much-needed night of sleep!

The Marine Band led a parade of workmen from the Philadelphia Navy Yard on April 4, 1865, when news arrived in Philadelphia that Richmond had fallen.

One of the first optimistic moments for Washingtonians was the arrival in the nation's capital of the 7th New York, April 25, 1861, as this famous regiment, led by its magnificent band, passed along Pennsylvania Avenue to the White House to pay respects to the newly-inaugurated President.

Confederate surrender in the field as news of Capital's fall reaches them.

New York bands were among the best in the East. The band of the 79th New York "Highlanders," composed entirely of professional musicians, was so good that it was constantly being called on to instruct and drill the "country" bands which accompanied new regiments to the field. The band of the 79th New York "Highlanders" gave a fine concert in the Washington Theater for the

The nation mourns the death of President Lincoln in 1865.

benefit of the widows and orphans who fell at Bull Run; the house was packed on the occasion (August 7, 1861), and a substantial amount was raised for this worthy cause.

Of the bands that came within hearing distance of the 11th N.H. at one time or another, the one enlisted with the 103rd N.Y., was by far the best. A bass and tenor drum and six brass instruments—eight men only —made up the band. Every man was a German and each an accomplished soloist on his particular instrument.

Early in the war, the only New Jersey regiment to have a brass band was the 6th New Jersey Infantry. This regiment had "music a-plenty; a band, 15 drummers and five fifers."

At the beginning of the war, brass bands were considered essential to every regiment. This was particularly true in the East. States like Massachusetts made every effort to have bands accompany their regiments to the field in 1861 and 1862. Often it was possible to get the services of such established musi-

cal organizations as Hodge's Band of North Adams, one of the most famous in the western portion of the state of Massachusetts.

In the formation of regiments, the old militia officers frequently played a prominent part. Often there was a good deal of old-fashioned bass drumming, parading in single-file formation, and training on every open lot throughout the village or town. A kind of martial enthusiasm was thereby engendered which was a temporary substitute for the grimmer realities of soldiering soon to come. Some of the old militia musicians, devoid of real musical ability, hastened to enlist during the early months of the war. Some enlisted from sincere patriotic motives; some, however, enlisted for the state bounties.

As the historian of the 23rd Massachusetts Infantry put it:

Certain men, such as could afford to leave their civilian occupations for the enlisted men's pay, and were, in their own estimation, capable of earning that pay as musicians, had collected at

Virginia troops, en route for Manasses Junction, crossing the Blue Ridge at daybreak.

Sailors aboard ship. (U.S. Signal Corps Brady collection from the National Archives)

. . . [camp]. When . . . [these men were] put to trial, . . . some of them were utterly incapable. These were summarily sent to their homes. A successful search was made for qualified musicians; the regimental officers agreed to contribute to extra pay for the band members, and a good band was organized which performed with credit.

Sometimes men objected to the cost of their band. The 44th Massachusetts Infantry hired the Boston Brass Band but the men were not consulted and resented being assessed for the cost. It was suggested that "a few of our rich friends in Boston" should get together and defray the cost. Eventually instruments were donated for the band and the men were very curious to see them. The lieutenant colonel of the regiment, with no imagination, ordered that no person would

be permitted to enter the band area except band members on penalty of punishment. This order caused much resentment but the order was strictly enforced.

Germans were very popular as band leaders. In January 1862, the 19th Massachusetts Infantry band had just received a new band leader—a Mr. Reinbach of the Germania Band of Boston. Reinbach played a B♭ cornet, and, according to a band member, played it "smart," was "full of music and running over."

Regimental bands were often brought in part or completely from civilian bands already in existence. Many of these civilian organizations were well known in their home state, and some, like Gilmore's Band,

Union troops parade, on Pennsylvania Avenue in the Grand Review of the armies on May 23-24, 1865, to celebrate Johnny's homecoming.

New Hampshire Infantry in July 1864, his place was taken by a French citizen musician of New Orleans, James Maurepas, who served faithfully during the remainder of the war. Maurepas went to New Hampshire with the band at the end of the war, and then returned to Louisiana.

Pennsylvania sent several very fine bands to the front. Certainly much of the excellence of their music was due to the high proportion of German-Americans in these bands. These Germans were especially skilled in brass instruments, just as their countrymen are in other parts of the world. Among the Pennsylvania bands were: The Pennsylvania Cornet Band, 14 pieces, which served with the 21st Regiment, having been financed by contributions from the citizens of Philadelphia. The 65th Regimental Band played at the time of Lee's surrender, while the 75th Regimental Band from Philadelphia became very proficient in squad, company, regimental, and batallion drill, under the leadership of Rudolph Wittig. The 88th, 90th, 95th, 98th, and 106th Pennsylvania Volunteers had bands with members ranging in numbers from 17 to 24. All were mustered

enjoyed a national reputation. However, most bands were local units as, for example, the Nashua Cornet Band. This outfit established in April 1861, was mustered into the 9th New Hampshire Infantry on August 9, 1862. The men were assigned to line companies with the understanding that they would be detailed as a regimental band.

At least one Frenchman led a Yankee band. When the band leader left the 14th

Forty-fourth New York Infantry. On dress parade. (U.S. Signal Corps Brady collection from the National Archives)

The drum major of the First Virginia, April 1861. Bands played while the troops prepared for battle. He was C.R.M. Pohie.

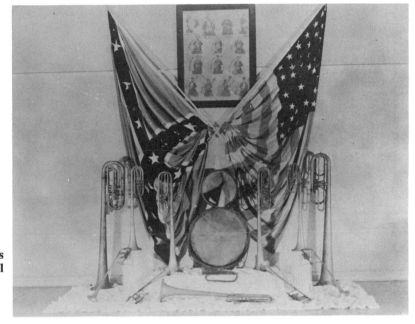

Virginia brass band with back firing instruments that went over the shoulder, from Stonewall Jackson's Staunton, Virginia band.

The Guthrie Grays, marching through Cincinnati en route for Camp Dennison. (Sketch by Mr. Noble)

Bandsmen at Ringold Barracks, 1864. (From National Archives)

**Band on Lookout Mountain, Tennessee, about 1864.
(Photo by Robert M. Linn. From the State Historical Society, Wisconsin)**

Indiana 44th Drummer, Company "H" Infantry. (From the U.S. Signal Corps photo, Brady collection, National Archives)

out in the fall of 1862. But it was a Pennsylvania regimental band, the 114th Regiment or Collis' Zouaves, which was the only Federal band that remained in service, intact, for the entire duration of the war. Apparently other bands in Federal service also enlisted for the duration, but their membership changed from time to time.

The formation of the several Philadelphia regiments in the three-months' service included the enlistment of many of the best military musicians in the city. In some cases the pay for these musicians was borne by the regimental officers. Associations of patriotic citizens subscribed to enable favorite regi-

ments to keep numerically strong bands in the field. When the short-term regiments came home and recruiting became active for three years' regiments, nearly all of the best bandsmen re-enlisted.

Among the three year regiments was the 114th Pennsylvania Infantry (Collis' Zouaves), which not only had a brass band, but also a drum corps and a vivandiere to accompany the men to the front.

The band of the 104th Pennsylvania Infantry was composed of young Germans who became very proficient in their band music. The band of the 93rd Pennsylvania Infantry was called the "Perseverance Band" in honor of the Perseverance Fire Company of Lebanon, Pennsylvania, whose members made up the regimental band. It was known as the

Brass band and drums. (From the George Eastman house of Rochester, New York)

"93rd Regiment Band" which designation was inscribed on its bass drum. According to the regimental history, this band had the prestige of being in continuous military service through the Civil War, and its reputation for military music remains undimmed and its excellence as a musical organization (1911) is unsurpassed.

The leader of the band of the 9th Connecticut Infantry was Christian Streit who had served in the German Army. An accomplished musician, Streit had long been a member of the New Haven City Band. He, and his 24 fellow musicians, were discharged on September 17, 1862.

Other Eastern states, like Maine, Rhode Island, and Vermont, had good bands. Al-most without exception all these bands consisted of between 23-24 musicians under a leader or "principal musician." The 5th West Virginia Cavalry under Principal Musician John R. Thomas had one of the best bands in the service. Prior to the war this band participated in a great Republican parade in Pittsburgh during the 1860 presidential campaign and was conceded to be the best civilian band present on that occasion. It was organized as a regimental band for active military service during the war.

REGIMENTAL BANDS IN THE WEST

The Western armies apparently had fewer bands than were present in the Eastern armies. Even as late as the "Grand Review" in Washington in May 1865, Sherman's armies had to hire several civilian bands to

Private Varney, Co. "A," 12th regiment. (From the National Archives)

Bandsmen of the Fourth Michigan Infantry who came from the West in their tasseled caps to fight for the Union cause.

furnish music for them during the parade down Pennsylvania Avenue.

Western bands often differed from Eastern bands in several interesting particulars. For example, some bands were led by commissioned officers rather than enlisted men. The 40th Ohio Infantry was headed by a first lieutenant, assisted by a first sergeant, two sergeants, and three corporals. There were an additional seven privates in the band.

Some regiments had their band members divided into three "classes" as for example, the 50th Illinois Infantry. This band of 16 men had a leader, 4 first class, 6 second class, and 5 third class musicians.

And, occasionally the service of the Western bands was a rather abbreviated one. Among such was the 31st Indiana Infantry which had a band of 15 members most of whom were mustered out of the service on September 8, 1862. They had served about one year.

The 6th Indiana Infantry had a band of 18 musicians, almost all were of German extraction, who enlisted in September-October 1861 and were discharged in May 1862, after about 8 months' service.

The 1st Minnesota Infantry band, 23 men, was formed on April 29, 1861, but served only four months and was then mustered out.

Band in the foreground. The 35th Abbeville, South Carolina volunteers in front of the fashionable Charleston, South Carolina hotel.

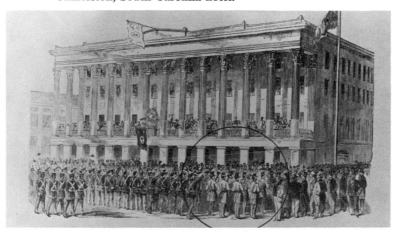

Several regiments had excellent bands. Among these was the band of the 4th Minnesota Infantry whose splendid band often played music which revived the men's spirits. The music gave them courage to push on over dusty roads on long marches when the men were ready to collapse and give up.

Another regiment, the 6th Iowa Infantry, had a band from its very muster into the service. After Shiloh it was reorganized as the Regimental Silver Cornet Band and "discoursed music of a high excellence" — and soon became popular throughout the division. When the band was disbanded there was sincere regret on the part of every soldier in the regiment. Nearly all the band members were first class musicians who took great pride in the organization and their reputation as musicians and soldiers. The enlisted men detailed as musicians in the band were ordered back to their companies.

It was customary with Federal armies in the West, that when a company had re-

For new recruits, drums and a parade.

Bailey's cross roads review, November 20, 1861. General McClellan reviewed 70,000 men. A typical band is in the foreground.

Twenty-third Infantry. (From the National Archives) 45

enlisted three-fourths of its men, it would parade through the company streets, headed by the regimental fife and drums corps. Everybody would cheer, and soon the men in the other companies of the regiment would begin to line up to re-enlist.

Some Western regiments were not too well favored with music. For instance, the 1st Tennessee Cavalry had only a "chief bugler." Probably the "prize" of all hopeless organizations was a Western band serving in the East. This was the band of the 6th Wisconsin Infantry of the famous "Iron Brigade." A survivor of the regiment has left us his impressions of the band:

It was enough to try the patience of a martyr, the performance of that contemptible brass band of ours. They played such slow time music that we passed the reviewing officer at about forty-seven paces a minute. We had to hold one leg in the air and balance on the other while we waited for the music . . . [the band is so bad that] if a man in the regiment is caught in a rascally trick, the whole regiment yells "put him in the brass band."

However, the regiment *was* proud of the drum major William Whaley, whose "lofty pomposity" so impressed General McClellan at a mammoth review that the General took off his hat as Whaley strutted past at the head of the band. But Whaley was so overcome by this recognition which took place while he "was indulging in a top loftical

Soldier's Ball, Huntsville, Alabama.

Electrifying news, April 3, 1865 sweeps through the North. Parades and bands came into life from nowhere.

gyration of his baton" that he dropped the baton! From the heights of glory poor Whaley was plunged into the deepest gulf of despair.

FEDERAL MOUNTED BANDS

Some regiments had mounted bands. Among these were the 65th and 70th Pennsylvania Infantry, connected to cavalry regiments. The 70th became the famous Rush Lancers. On January 1, 1862, to the music of their splendid mounted band, the Lancers, nearly 1,000 strong, paraded through Washington.

A regimental band for the 11th New York Cavalry was organized by detailing men who had, or who pretended they had, musical ability. During the winter 1861-1862 they made a fair degree of progress. Their intentions were well meant, but they had the usual objections that accompany a new band — something out of harmony. The band was mounted on dun-colored horses which became proficient in tactics long before their riders did in music. But Orpheus eventually breathed upon them and they soon could play. The band was involuntarily disbanded

on the 29th of June 1864, at Reams Station.

The 4th Iowa Cavalry had a 17-member brass band composed of men regularly enlisted in the various companies. While at Helena, Arkansas, this band was mustered out in 1862 in order to permit one band for the entire division. But in 1863, due to the soldiers' love of band music, a private brass band was organized. By subscription among officers and men, a set of instruments was purchased and the men who undertook to play them were encouraged to do so by being relieved of fatigue duty. The men served until muster out of the regiment, but great difficulty was encountered in getting time to practice, because these men had to serve in the line during active operations.

FEDERAL COLORED BANDS

There were a few bands organized among the Negro regiments raised for Federal service. In the famous 54th Massachusetts Infantry the senior officers raised five hundred dollars for the purchase of instruments for the regimental band. This band was instructed by a musician from the 48th New York Infantry, a white regiment.

3. Federal Brigade Bands

After the issuance of the War Department order for mustering out of service the regimental bands, a new band organization came into being. This was the brigade band. Frequently, members of the disbanded regimental bands, whose enlistment service had not expired, were detailed to serve in these newly-constituted brigade organizations. In the case of the 9th New Hampshire, this was done by a circular issued October 1, 1862, by Headquarters, First Brigade, Second Division, 9th Army Corps. Such detailed men were now safe from being put back in the ranks, but they really earned their private's salary. They had to be present at guard mounting, dress parades, general inspections, brigade drills, Sunday service, and serenades of high officers; and often these serenades were arduous affairs. For example, on March 11, 1865, General Samuel D. Sturgis kept the band playing at his quarters from 8 o'clock in the evening til 2 o'clock the next morning!

Before a battle, brigade bands reported to the division surgeon who put them to work, cutting pine and cedar boughs for the wounded, setting up field hospitals and similar preparations. After the fighting was over, some bandsmen were detailed to cook for the wounded while others took stretchers and moved out to the battle lines, bringing in friend and foe alike.

An interesting but macabre duty of brigade bands was their frequent playing at the executions of deserters. This was especially true from the fall of 1863 to the end of the war.

Rehearsals were kept up religiously. For example, a brigade band in the 9th Army Corps received orders December 14, 1864, that after guard mount in the morning each man should practice by himself for one hour, that at 2 P.M. the full band should play at headquarters for one and a half hours, and at 4 P.M. the band should play for dress parade. Moreover, after the parade, "a few pieces" had to be played in front of the brigade commander's quarters, and that evening rehearsals should last from 6 to 8 P.M. making a total of 7½ hours per day for each man.

On the rainy morning of April 10th (1865), just as a brigade band of the 9th Army Corps was trying to decide whether to play or not, an aide dashed up to the general's quarters with the news of Lee's surrender. The aide called out to the members of the band, "Boys, can't you give us a little music!" The boys rather thought they could, and amid cheers, din, and confusion indescribable,

Sutlers' PX opened their well stocked stores to sell the soldiers extra comforts such as tobacco, cigars, candy, magazines and even a bottle of whiskey.

Sailors on board ship. (From the Western Reserve collection, Cleveland, Ohio) Music in the navy was very scarce.

Headquarters of General Wright at Fort Walker, Hilton Head, South Carolina, formerly those of General Drayton of the Rebel Army. Drummer boy on the left. (From Harper's November 30, 1861)

Song sheets of the North. (From the collection of Norm Flayderman of Greenwich, Connecticut)

played for two solid hours, winding up with the national airs and "Yankee Doodle." The Johnnies, many of whom were prisoners near by, were no less glad that peace had come.

Sometimes a civilian band entered the service as a brigade band. Such was the case in the Second Vermont Brigade, whose new band of 17 pieces was organized under the direction of a Mr. Clark from St. Johnsbury, Mr. Clark's concerts in Vermont had won state-wide recognition.

The regimental band of the 11th New Hampshire Infantry stayed on and, in October 1862, was organized as a brigade band. Members furnished their own instruments and drew the pay of privates.

A famous brigade band was Stewart's Band of the 4th Brigade, 2nd Division, 6th Army Corps. This band went everywhere the 6th Corps went; at the Battle of the Wilderness its members were ordered to assist the surgeons at the division hospital. In all the hard fought battles of the Army of the Potomac, from the Wilderness to Petersburg, the band assisted the surgeons. On the march it accompanied Brigade Headquarters.

The band leader of the 7th Ohio Infantry band was mustered out with the entire band

July 5, 1862. Over two years later (September 16, 1864) he re-entered the service as leader of the band for the 2nd Brigade, 3rd Division, 23rd Army Corps, and served throughout the rest of the war.

The First Brigade of U.S. Colored Troops, composed of the 1st Alabama Infantry "of African descent" and the 1st West Virginia Infantry, also "of African descent," had their own brigade band.

On June 10, 1865, the Adjutant General's Office ordered that when brigades were broken up due to muster out of regiments of those brigades, the brigade bands should also be mustered out.

On August 2, 1864, near Atlanta, Georgia, five men were discharged from the Brigade Band for "physical disability and ignorance of music."

Occupations of Brigade Band, 3rd Brigade, 2nd Division, 21st Army Corps:

Confederate water battery, Pensacola, shows drum being used for firing of guns. (From National Archives, Chief of Engineers)

1 barber	3 clerks
1 bridge builder	1 engineer
1 blacksmith	2 watch makers
1 farmer	1 printer
1 laborer	1 school teacher
1 artist	1 jeweler
1 pilot	

These 16 men were discharged from their regiments so they could be mustered into the Band at Cripple Creek, Tenn.

By special Order No. 100, Adjutant General's Office, February 28, 1865, all members of Brigade Bands who had been transferred to the Veterans Reserve Corps, and who were presently in that corps, were, upon a proper medical examination, found to be unfit for further field duty, to be discharged from the U.S. Service.

February 20, 1864—list of clothing issued to Band, 2nd Brigade, 3rd Division, 6th Corps:

1 pr. trousers, infantry	1 canteen
2 knit shirts	1 haversack
2 pr. flannel drawers	1 knapsack
3 pr. stockings	2 great coat straps

Twenty-second New York Infantry with drummer boy standing full length in uniform. (From National Archives, U.S. Signal Corps, Brady collection)

B-5497

Winter quarters. Notice the youth of the drummer boy, the various type of shelters used for the winter quarters. The barrel on the roof is an important improvised chimney. (From the National Archives)

Confederates of '61 of May 10th, from the Georgia Volunteer Infantry with drummer boys in the center.

Old Vet drums. A.H. Haynes, J.J. Lewis, W.T. Johnson and W.D. Smith of L.O'B Branch Drum Corps with the only old vet drums in existence. (Louisville, Kentucky, 1905 State Department of Archives, Raleigh, North Carolina)

Shivering drummers, some mere boys, line up in the icy dawn to beat out reveille.

1 great coat   1 rubber blanket
1 woolen blanket

The following Brigade Bands have been identified in the National Archives. It must be emphasized that this list is not necessarily a complete one. Moreover, the same band may be found in more than one brigade because the brigade itself may have been assigned to various divisions during its service.

1st Brigade, 1st Division, 1st Army Corps
1st Brigade, 1st Division, 2nd Army Corps
2nd Brigade, 1st Division, 2nd Army Corps
3rd Brigade, 3rd Division, 2nd Army Corps
2nd Brigade, 3rd Division, 4th Army Corps
1st Brigade, 1st Division, 6th Army Corps
2nd Brigade, 1st Division, 6th Army Corps
3rd Brigade, 1st Division, 6th Army Corps
1st Brigade, 2nd Division, 6th Army Corps
3rd Brigade, 2nd Division, 6th Army Corps
4th Brigade, 2nd Division, 6th Army Corps
2nd Brigade, 3rd Division, 6th Army Corps
1st Brigade, 1st Division, 7th Army Corps
1st Brigade, 1st Division, 9th Army Corps

2nd Brigade, 1st Division, 9th Army Corps
3rd Brigade, 1st Division, 9th Army Corps
2nd Brigade,   Division, 10th Army Corps
1st Brigade, 1st Division, 13th Army Corps
3rd Brigade, 1st Division, 14th Army Corps
1st Brigade, 3rd Division, 14th Army Corps
2nd Brigade, 4th Division, 14th Army Corps
1st Brigade, 2nd Division, 15th Army Corps
3rd Brigade, 2nd Division, 15th Army Corps
1st Brigade,   Division, 15th Army Corps
1st Brigade, 1st Division, 16th Army Corps
1st Brigade, 1st Division, 17th Army Corps
3rd Brigade, 1st Division, 17th Army Corps
1st Brigade, 2nd Division, 17th Army Corps
    Brigade, 1st Division, 18th Army Corps
1st Brigade, 3rd Division, 19th Army Corps
2nd Brigade, 1st Division, 20th Army Corps
3rd Brigade, 2nd Division, 21st Army Corps
1st Brigade,   Division, 22nd Army Corps
2nd Brigade, 3rd Division, 23rd Army Corps
2nd Brigade, 4th Division, 23rd Army Corps
    Brigade, 1st Division, 24th Army Corps
3rd Brigade, 3rd Division, 24th Army Corps
3rd Brigade, 2nd Division (Eastport, Miss.)
2nd Brigade, 1st Division, Army of the Miss.
1st Brigade, 1st Division, Army of the
    Shenandoah
1st Brigade, 1st Division, Army of the Frontier

The drummer boy, in midst of the battle and the outcome.

Drummer boys in camp duty.

Hazen's Brigade, Army of the Cumberland
Michigan Brigade
Davidson's Brigade (St. Louis, Missouri)
3rd Brigade, 3rd Division (Huntsville, Ala.)
Kenley's Brigade Band
Brigade Band, Norfolk, Va.
Davis' Brigade, Folly Island, S. C.
Brigade Band, Harpers Ferry, W. Va.
1st Brigade, 1st Division, Cavalry Corps
2nd Brigade, 3rd Division, Cavalry Corps
Engineer Brigade

Depot Band, Fort Columbus, N. Y.
Post Band, Governor's Island, N. C.
Artillery School, Fort Monroe, Va.
    Colored Bands:
1st Brigade, Corps d'Afrique
2nd Brigade, Corps d'Afrique
1st Brigade, 2nd Division, (Port Hudson, La.)
1st Brigade, U.S. Colored Troops
    (Baltimore, Md.)
Headquarters, Department of the Cumberland,
    Nashville, Tenn.

The Plain Drum. (Chicago Historical Society, 9th Regiment Vermont Volunteers) Drum in photo individually painted.

4. Confederate Bands

If references to Federal bands are comparatively few, those to Confederate bands are fewer still. Unquestionably, there were Confederate bands. But, due to the lack of trained musicians, band instruments, and above all, the necessity to put all available men into line units, it was extremely difficult to organize and maintain bands in Confederate front line units. However, the Confederates partially compensated for their lack of band music by a very general participation, by all ranks, in vocal and improvised instrumental music. Many regiments had glee clubs, violinists, guitarists, and banjoists.

Jeb Stuart delighted to have his famous banjo player, Sweeney, in his tent. Even while busily engaged in official correspondence, the General called for Sweeney to play and sing some favorite ditty, such as "Jine the Cavalry."

On December 10, 1861, the Confederate Congress enacted that the President was authorized to appoint a chief bugler or principal musician, according to corps, to each regiment in the Provisional Army.

A few months later (April 15, 1862), the Confederate Congress enacted a law whereby all colored persons employed as musicians in any regiment or company were entitled to the same pay allowed by law to regularly enlisted musicians. Provided, however, that no such persons would be employed as musicians without the consent of the commanding officer of the brigade to which said regiments or companies belonged.

It is significant that the Confederate Government, fully aware of the need for every fighting man to be available for combat duty, provided in Section 75, Article XII of the 1863 Regulations that:

The musicians of the band will, for the time being, be dropped from the company muster-rolls, but they will be instructed as soldiers, and liable to serve in the ranks on any occasion. They will be mustered in a separate squad under the chief musician, with the non-commissioned staff, and be included in the aggregate in all regimental returns.

In Section 76, it was provided that:

When a regiment occupies several stations, the band will be kept at the headquarters, provided troops (one or more companies) be serving there. The field music belonging to companies not stationed at regimental headquarters, will not be separated from their respective companies.

Of lesser interest to us, perhaps, but of very real concern to the men involved, was the following: (Section 110, Article XII, 1863 Regulations):

Stonewall Jackson at the battle of Bull Run.

"Jimmy" Dugan was a bugler boy in the band at Carlisle barracks, Pennsylvania. He was one of the boys who made good soldiers.

Messes will be prepared by privates of squads, including private musicians, each taking his turn. The greatest care will be observed in washing and scouring the cooking utensils; those made of brass and copper should be lined with tin.

The *Regulations* failed to mention how lowly bandsmen in the field could accomplish this with the meager means at hand!

A famous Confederate band with an active post-war service was the Stonewall Brigade Band of Staunton, Virginia. As late as 1900 there were 38 members of this band, six of them original members of the 1861-1865 period, and the remainder were all sons of veterans. This band, organized in 1855, was originally known as the "Mountain Saxhorn Band" and retained this name until mustered in as the 5th Virginia Regiment Band in 1861. The band was soon organized into a "Surgeon Corps" and soon won the respect and gratitude of the men of the Stonewall Brigade for their assistance to the wounded during the many battles of that excellent organization.

At Appomattox, General Grant issued an order permitting the members of the band to take their instruments home with them.

Many years after the war these instruments were on proud exhibition in the band's hall; they were probably the only complete set of Civil War band instruments in existence by the turn of the century. These instruments were exhibited by the band during their engagement at the World's Fair in Chicago as well as at reunions. The band was able to express its appreciation of Grant's kindness to them at the occasion of the General's funeral in New York, where the band occupied a post of honor.

In the *Confederate Veteran* for October 1901, J. W. Blaker tells us how the "Valley Brass Band" of the 48th Virginia Infantry obtained a furlough, flanked the pickets, and went some twenty miles in disputed territory to visit their homes. To get their furlough the bandsmen serenaded General Lee and each commanding general in the corps down to their regimental commander! The music had the desired effect and the furloughs came back approved. On their trip homeward the men were stopped by order of General Early who had issued

Drummer boys, and Union troops on the march.

orders forbidding any soldiers to pass his lines. The bandsmen laughingly pointed out that *they* had not heard that Early outranked Lee. They continued on their way, and despite the presence of Federals throughout their home stay, they returned safely to their camp. The Valley Brass Band had been organized before the war; it enlisted as a body and was permitted to retain its instruments after the surrender at Appomattox.

The bandmaster of the 4th Kentucky Infantry band, Charles Ward, was a composer as well as a musician. His "Old Play Ground" was considered to be one of the finest antebellum songs written by an American.

According to the *Confederate Veteran* for November 1903, the 43rd Mississippi Infantry had a camel named "Old Douglas." This animal was assigned to the regimental band for whom it carried knapsacks and band instruments. When the regiment was ready to move out on a march, Old Douglas would be led up to the pile of packs and instruments. His leader would then say:

The wounded drummer boy goes bravely on the shoulders of a comrade. (Frick Art Reference Library, New York City)

The city of Montgomery, Alabama, showing the State House where the Congress met on February 4, 1861.

Drummer boys, of the 8th Regiment of the National Guard of the State of New York.

Presentation of colors to the 20th United States Colored Infantry, Colonel Bertram, New York City.

Drummers of the field band of the 2nd Infantry.
(From the National Archives)

Drummer boy of Shiloh, General Clem, was 12 in
1863. (From National Archives, U.S. Signal Corps,
Brady collection)

**Battle of Bull Run, Virginia, fought July 21, 1861
commanded by McDowell and Beauregard.**

Feb. 22. 1861 -

Lincoln at Philadelphia on his way to Washington.
(Harper's)

Zouaves, from Charleston, and a drum.

"Pushay, Douglas," and the camel would drop to his knees and haunches and hold that position until loaded. His long swinging gait was a familiar sight and the 43rd became known as the "Camel Regiment."

In the two days prior to the surprise of Grant's Army at Shiloh, the Confederates could plainly hear the Federal drums and bands playing. The Confederates never ceased to wonder how they were permitted by the enemy to remain within hearing distance of the music for about two whole days and nights and not be discovered.

Certainly one of the queerest drum majors of the Civil War (or any war) was to be found in the band of the 3rd Mississippi Infantry. Many of the men had pets, among which was an old gander owned by Musi-

cian Fink, a trombone player. This gander had been brought to camp in the fall of 1862 by a visitor who intended to sell the bird for eating purposes. But since the gander was about 30 years old, Fink decided to adopt it as a pet. The first time Fink took his trombone out for practice, the gander walked along in perfect time to the music. So Fink clipped his wings and allowed him the freedom of the camp. Soon this gander began to appear at regimental and brigade reviews at the head of the 3rd Mississippi band! The bird marched "with a very soldierly air," swinging its head from right to left as if observing his surroundings with great interest, and would wag its tail to the time of the music with as much precision as a drum major would wield a baton.

On the march to Gettysburg, Rode's Division was pushing forward but it was very hot and the men all but exhausted. Noticing this, Lee rode up to the head of Dale's Brigade and ordered the band of the 4th Georgia Infantry to play for the men. The music "had a most exhilarating effect"; the men stepped out briskly, inspired both by the interest of their commander and the strains of "Tom, March On" by the band.

As late as the disastrous battle of Franklin, November 30, 1864, Confederate bands were playing during actual combat. In the *Confederate Veteran* for February 1911, S. C. Trigg of the 3rd Missouri Infantry relates one such incident. He and his comrades of Cockrill's Brigade expected a walkover in their attack on the Federal position:

Seeing the nice, smooth field between us and the enemy's works . . . [Trigg] with many others called on the Colonel for music and for a brigade drill. To this he readily consented and so ordered. Soon the band began to play and

continued until the enemy's batteries began to rake our lines. One man was killed before the music ceased.

(Presumably, this man was from the 3rd Missouri band). However, in the same issue of the *Confederate Veteran*, T. B. Yeates of the 28th Tennessee Infantry insisted that *his* band was the one who played at Franklin. Yeates was on detail with the skirmishers of his regiment. As they charged forward, they heard a band playing "Dixie." A wounded comrade of Yeates exclaimed: "My God, listen to that band!" Yeates turned to see what band was playing, only to discover it was from his own regiment. The editor of

Drums and troops on the charge.

The review or parade with a drum corps up front.

the *Confederate Veteran* hinted that several bands played during the Confederate charge at Franklin. According to Captain Joseph Boyce (*Confederate Veteran* June 1911), Cockrell's Brigade had one of the best brass bands in the Confederate Army. This band moved out with the infantry in their charge, playing the "Bonnie Blue Flag," but changing to "Dixie" as they neared the enemy.

A very unique source is a recent publication based on the Civil War diary of Julius Auguştus Leinbach (1834-1930), who served as musician in the regimental band of the 26th North Carolina Infantry, C.S.A.

This band was one of the best Confederate bands; "their performances evoked nothing but the highest praise from soldier and civilian alike." The organization, one of the oldest bands in the United States, was composed of Moravians from Salem, North Carolina. This town had a band from 1831. But when the Civil War broke out, two other

North Carolina regiments (the 11th and 33rd) had departed with their bands before the 26th finally enlisted in March 1862.

The Salem Brass Band, thus enlisted in Confederate service as the regimental band for the 26th North Carolina Infantry, was originally composed of the following:

Samuel T. Mickey (leader) E♭ cornet
A. P. Gibson   1st B♭ cornet
Joe O. Hall   2nd B♭ cornet
Augustus Hauser   1st E♭ alto
William H. Hall   2nd E♭ alto
Daniel T. Crouse   1st B♭ tenor
Alexander C. Meinung   2nd B♭ tenor
Julius A. Leinbach   E♭ bass

Though small in number, this group lacked only a drum to complete its remarkably balanced brass band instrumentation.

Many Confederates in 1861 took their favorite instruments to camp with them, including flutes, banjos, and violins.

While some Confederate units had little or no music, others had regimental bands, occasionally as many as two or three to a brigade. However, the great difficulty in getting instruments, the scarcity of trained musicians, and the ever-present need for every able-bodied man in the ranks, resulted in a paucity of good bands in the Confederate service.

General Lee himself, after listening to a serenade of a brass band, remarked: "I don't

Reveille, after an anxious night at the front. (Ad Worthing & Co. of Hartford, Connecticut)

Union troops on parade as they leave for the front, drums always present.

Self entertainment. (From the Frick Art Reference Library, New York)

THE SOLDIER IN OUR CIVIL WAR.

Recruiting in Philadelphia for the famous Bucktail Regiment, the 1st Pennsylvania Reserve.

**Paying off soldiers at Atlanta, Georgia, before
starting on the Grand March to the sea.**

69

Bugler closing the arms & trophies department for the day.

Weapons and equipment on display. (From the Flayderman collection)

believe we can have an army without music." This was in 1864.

In contrast with Federal serenading groups, the Confederates were often forced to use any type of musical instrument available—and, in weird combinations—when they serenaded the high-ranking officers. Whereas the Federals could furnish a well-balanced, highly trained brass band, the Confederates often would have to combine brass instruments with violins or guitars.

Many Confederate units put on amateur theatricals for the amusement of their fellow soldiers. Music was usually furnished on such occasions. One of the most celebrated theatrical groups in the Confederate service was to be found in the famous Washington Artillery of New Orleans. This unit presented exceptionally fine variety shows during the winter lull between active campaigns. Programs were printed in Richmond and widely distributed among soldiers and civilians alike. Generals in their best uniforms shared seats with privates, some of whom came on foot from distances as much

as twenty miles away. Music was furnished by the combined bands of the 12th and 16th Mississippi Infantry.

When General W. F. Smith's Confederate brigade entered York, Pennsylvania, in mid-June, 1863, he ordered up "those tooting fellows" as he called his brigade band, and had them play "Yankee Doodle." The General, riding alone in front, bowed and saluted first to one side and then the other, especially to every pretty girl he saw!

A British officer with Lee's army during the Gettysburg campaign (Lt. Col. Arthur J. L. Freemantle) recorded the following on June 27th:

I entered Chambersburg [Pennsylvania] at 6 P.M. . . . The natives were in the streets, or at the upper windows, looking in a scowling and bewildered manner at the Confederate troops, who were marching gayly past to the tune of "Dixie's Land." The women (many of whom were pretty and well dressed) were particularly sour and disagreeable in their remarks. I heard one of them say, "Look at Pharaoh's army going to the Red Sea." . . . [but the men, dirty and ragged] were full of good-humour and confidence in themselves and in their general, Hood. They answered the numerous taunts of the

Memorial parade. The annual one perhaps in the 1900's. (From Philadelphia Library Print Division)

Playing soldier and the veteran, many years after the conflict.

Chambersburg ladies with cheers and laughter. One female had seen fit to adorn her ample bosom with a huge Yankee flag, and she stood at the door of her house, her countenance expressing the utmost contempt for the barefooted Rebs; several companies passed her without taking any notice, but at length a Texan gravely remarked, "Take care, madam, for Hood's boys are great at storming breastworks when the Yankee colours is on them." After this speech the patriotic lady made a precipitate retreat.

Washington saw a queer sight on Friday,

April 7, 1865. A Confederate band serenaded Secretary of War Stanton. The band members, bearing their instruments, were part of an arriving boatload of Confederate deserters. As soon as they landed, the musicians began to play; in fact, so great was the novelty that traffic was stopped at the War Department by the delighted crowds. The band did not play Federal music but such tunes as "Dixie," "Jordan," and "Ain't we glad to get out of the Wilderness." On Stan-

Union troops singing "Glory Hallelujah."

ton's behalf, Adjutant General E. D. Townsend welcomed the deserting musicians, several of whom expressed regret that they were unable to play the national airs!

A day or two after Lee's surrender in April 1865, four Federal naval officers celebrating in Richmond gathered around a piano in one of the abandoned houses and began some quartette singing. Out of deference to some paroled Confederate officers in a nearby house, no patriotic songs were sung. However, a note soon arrived from the Confederates, asking permission to come over and listen to the singing. Among the officers

was a high-ranking general officer of the Confederacy. After introductions, the Federals sang a series of glee club and college songs. Finally, the General said "Excuse me, gentlemen, you sing delightfully but what we want to hear is your army songs." Then the Federals sang several favorites, including the "Battle Hymn of the Republic", "John Brown's Body", "We're Coming, Father Abraham", "Tramp, Tramp, Tramp", and ending up with "Rally Round the Flag, Boys."

When the applause had subsided, a fine-looking Confederate major said "Gentlemen,

Camp scene, bugle, music and drums.

Thirty thousand volunteers with cash bounties being offered.

Display was seen at Gimbel's of Philadelphia, Pennsylvania, in 1962-63.

Bugle calls played a very important part in the
Civil War. They were unified in 1867 by General
Upton.

5. Tatto

6. Extinguish Lights

8. Sick

9. School

10. Church

11. Drill

"Pack Up"

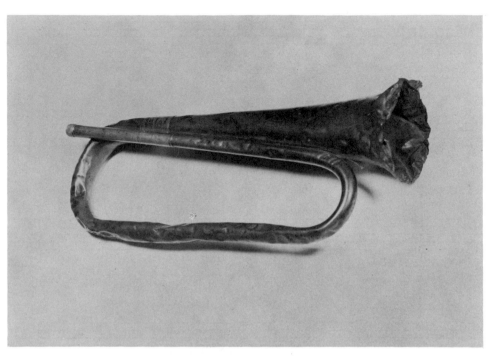

Bugle from the Stonewall Brigade.

if we'd had your songs, we'd have licked you out of your boots! Who couldn't have marched or fought with such songs? Why, we had nothing, absolutely nothing, except a bastard 'Marseillaise', the 'Bonnie Blue Flag' and 'Dixie', which was nothing but jigs. 'Maryland, My Maryland' was a splendid song, but . . . every one of these Yankee songs is full of marching and fighting spirit . . ." On parting, the General said "Well, the time may come when we can all sing the 'Star Spangled Banner' again."

A Confederate major in April 1865, in conversation with a group of Federal and Confederate officers, told about the first time he heard "Rally Round the Flag," an experience he never would forget:

It was a nasty night during the Seven Days Fight, and, if I remember rightly, it was raining. I was on picket, when, just before taps, some fellow on the other side struck up that song, and others joined in the chorus until it seemed to me the whole Yankee army was singing. Tom B—, who was with me, sung out, "Good heavens,

Cap, what are those fellows made of, anyway? Here we've licked 'em six days running and now, on the eve of the seventh they're singing 'Rally Round the Flag'. I am not naturally superstitious, but I tell you that song sounded to me like the "knell of doom" . . .

Due to lack of records, it is almost impossible to ascertain the exact number of instruments in the "average" Confederate band. Apparently the assortment of instruments and qualifications of the musicians varied widely. However, the *Regulations* of the Confederate Army (1861 and 1863), stipulated that:

When it is desired to have bands of music for regiments, there will be allowed for each, sixteen privates to act as musicians, in addition to the chief musicians authorized by law, provided, the total number of privates in the regiment, including the band, does not exceed the legal standard.

As with their counterparts in the Federal bands, bandsmen of Confederate organizations were usually assigned to assist the regimental surgeon behind the lines. They were put to work, assisting in dressing slight wounds as well as assisting the surgeons with more serious cases, including amputations. They carried water and wood, kept up the fires, and fed the helpless wounded. As the battle lines moved forward, the bandsmen followed the fighting men, evacuating the wounded by stretcher to the field hospitals.

5. Federal Fife and Drum Corps

In addition to a brass band, some regiments like the 25th Massachusetts Infantry, organized a drum corps. The 25th had a drum corps, composed of two musicians from each company, and instructed by the well known veteran drummer of Worcester; Jubal H. Haven. From early morning until late at night was heard the tapping of the sticks under the supervision of Drum Major Haven, whose skill at instructing was finally rewarded by an excellent drum corps. This drum corps remained with the regiment after the band had been discharged and sent home.

Sometimes the reverse was true. The 11th Rhode Island Infantry already had a fife and drum corps but "there was a desire for something still better, and it was decided to organize a brass band." The colonel headed a subscription list, followed by his officers and men; in two weeks nearly four hundred dollars, the amount required, was raised, and soon the brass band began regular practice.

It is interesting to note that veterans often complained after the war of the lack of publicity given to "field music" in the regimental histories. Writing his personal reminiscences in 1915, Enos B. Vail of the 20th New York pointed out:

I never read any work on the Civil War which mentioned anything about the Fife and Drum Corps. The Fife and Drum Corps constitute [ed] an important part of the army.

Vail's regiment had a fife and drum corps, consisting of a Drum "Instructor," a Drum Major, and 16 other musicians. Immediately after the Battle of Antietam, the position of Drum Major was abolished and all the regimental Drum Majors were discharged. It was soon evident that without a head, the musical part of the regiment would be practically useless. Then, Drummer James Pierce was appointed Principal Musician and Scotty was appointed Fife Major.

The duties of the Principal Musician were to see that all the calls were played at the proper time, make requisition for drum supplies, put in drum heads, and see that the instruments for which he was responsible were kept in order.

At sunrise, each morning, the calls were played in the following order: Drummers, reveille, breakfast, doctors, guard mount, dinner, supper, tattoo, and taps. In addition, there were calls for drill, and the whole corps turned out for dress parade.

The historian of the 17th Maine Infantry was quite poetic in his description of the role of the fife and drum corps:

As the first beams of the rising sun begin to

Backfiring instruments of the Civil War period, coming to this country in 1840 and disappearing around 1870. The brass family all had the same design.

Brigade band, Stonewall Jackson's of Staunton, Virginia.

Bugle of the 3rd Regiment, Virginia County which blew the charge at the battle of Bethel, Virginia, June 10, 1861. (Credit to Archives and History, Raleigh, North Carolina)

Headquarters band, involved in the Baxter Springs massacre incident of 1863. Photo is General James G. Blunt's band. (From Kansas State Historical Society)

tinge the eastern skies, the clear notes of the bugle, sounding reveille from head-quarters are heard—repeated in turn by the regimental buglers. The drums of one regiment commence their noisy rataplan, which is taken up by the "Ear piercing fife and spirit stirring drum" of another, which is in turn echoed by another, till every drum corps of the brigade, with accompanying bugles and fifes, join in the din, and the morning air is resonant with the rattle of drums, the shrill notes of the fife, or the clarion tones of the bugle, sounding reveille. At the last tap of the drum every man is supposed to be "up and dressed" the companies are formed, the roll called by the first sergeants, and woe to the absentees! "Extra duty" is the customary punishment of tardiness, and is the horror of a soldier.

The drum corps of each regiment, also known as the "field music," usually consisted of two musicians—a fifer and a tenor drummer—from each of the ten companies.

In the 148th Pennsylvania Infantry—the "Corn Exchange Regiment"—some of the men enlisted for the drum corps were poor musicians, while others preferred to serve in the ranks with muskets. Therefore, some men were detailed to the drum corps.

The indescribable lack of knowledge of military tactics of drum corps of the 148th Pennsylvania was very apparent during the first guard mount of the regiment. As the details from the companies of the regiment lined up for guard mount, the men of the drum corps began to straggle out to the parade ground. There was a complete lack of uniformity in the attire and equipment of the men detailed for the guard mount ceremony. Several of the men who "knew something about war" brought their weapons with them. Others, not apprehending any danger from prowling Confederates, came unarmed. Some were in shirt sleeves; others were attired in overcoats, dress coats, or blouses. The colonel was especially aghast at the appearance of the drum major who appeared for this formal ceremony in his shirt sleeves, completely devoid of equipment, and wearing a brilliantly colored sleeping cap on his head.

The equipment of the 148th Pennsylvania regimental drum corps was exceptionally well made. The colonel, scorning the ordinary contract issue of drums and fifes from the Government, procured instead a fine outfit of drums (including a basso profundo) and fifes from a Baltimore firm. The drums had the U.S. coat of arms and the regimental designation.

Although the drums corps of the 148th Pennsylvania Infantry got off to a slow start, it soon began to show the effects of drill and discipline. The music of this outfit attracted much attention from high-ranking

Band of the 9th Veteran Reserve Corps, Washington, D.C., April 1865. (Brady photo from the Library of Congress)

Band of the 114th Pennsylvania Infantry, Petersburg, Virginia. This band was quite famous and one of the few bands to serve the entire war. (A Brady photo from the Library of Congress)

Engineers musician, in full dress. (From the Smithsonian U.S. National Museum)

The Grand Review, on parade ground in which at least three bands can be seen.

Cincinnati Militia, their return with a brass band with backfiring instruments in the lead. (By H. Mosler)

officers and on January 7, 1863, the brigade commander, in a special order, decreed that the drum major of the 148th would take command of the musicians of the entire brigade for instruction and drill. Later, General Hancock ordered the Chief Musician of the 148th to take charge of the consolidated field music of the division whenever the troops paraded for drill or review.

According to a young fifer in the 103rd Ohio Infantry, his regiment had ten fifers and ten drummers, one of each to a company. The men were amateurs in every sense of the word. Soon after arrival at Frankfort, Kentucky, a dress parade was held. It was the musicians' part, after initial preliminaries to play a 4-4 march down the line, turn-around and play a quickstep back. On this occasion the 4-4 and 2-4 pieces were selected. The musicians arrived at the left of the line with no incident, about-faced, and started in the 2-4 quickstep. However, this was not true for all the musicians; the two fifers on the right were playing a 6-8 march! Because the snare drummers were young and inexperienced, this difference of time naturally confused them. They refused to tell what kind of time they did play. But the bass drummer said all this bothered him not at all. He explained that he beat 2-4 time with one hand and 6-8 with the other!

Musician, full dress, Artillery. (From the Smithsonian U.S. National Museum)

Full dress, Ordnance private. (From the Smithsonian U.S. National Museum)

6. Federal Buglers

Federal cavalry and artillery regiments had buglers but the number varied with different regiments. According to the historian of Battery "A," 1st Rhode Island Light Artillery, the cavalry and artillery units generally had only buglers for their military music. For example, on the march to First Bull Run (July 1861), " it was an inspiring scene to see the different (infantry) regiments filing into camp, and to hear the different drum corps beating tattoo, the artillery and cavalry buglers sounding the same call." The 7th Pennsylvania Cavalry had two "first buglers." One deserted and the other, after serving through the war, reenlisted in the Regular Army and was killed by Indians in an engagement in the West.

The 1st Rhode Island Cavalry had three "chief trumpeters," in addition to the company (troop) buglers and a band of musicians.

There was occasionally friction between the "old timers" and the newly recruited buglers in the volunteer regiments. This friction could take several forms.

Sometimes friction developed between the chief bugler and the company buglers. In the 17th Pennsylvania Cavalry the chief bugler was an old, regular army bugler, who

was an expert bugler and knew it. "He was proud as a peacock" and his ambition was to have the best group of buglers in the brigade. In this he succeeded, but he tended to be officious and too rigid in his discipline. Soon strained relations developed between him and one of the company buglers. "It was a contention between the regular army and the volunteer army." The chief bugler had no use for volunteers, and the company bugler had no use for regulars. Eventually this "impasse" was settled when the chief bugler and company bugler "took a walk" outside the guard line. When they returned, the company bugler, although heavier and taller than the chief bugler, seemed to have had the worst of the "walk." The company bugler accepted the verdict and told the colonel that he guessed the regular army regulations were right! But this didn't settle the matter; there was another "walk" later on. This time "volunteer regulations" won out. The colonel, exasperated at this constant bickering, told both regular and volunteer that if there was any more disagreement, both would be reduced to the ranks. Thereupon the two buglers shook hands, and after that they were the best of friends.

In a cavalry regiment, with the exception of the first sergeant, the bugler was possibly

Monument Square, Baltimore, Maryland, with troops on hand to quell an anticipated riot.

A Union band at a river's crossing, the 46th Pennsylvania. General Banks going from the Potomac to attack Jackson with the band on Virginia shore.

Reveille at dawn.

Infantry musician, in full dress. (From the Smithsonian U.S. National Museum)

the most conspicuous of all enlisted men. Nearly all the camps' services and regimental drills were directed by bugler calls. A cavalry regiment had 25 buglers, two in each company, and one chief bugler. The chief bugler ranked as a sergeant and was attached to the regimental non-commissioned staff. The company buglers were members of their respective companies but were also subject to the orders of the chief bugler.

The buglers had regular periods of practice under the instruction of the chief bugler

exactly as line companies had drill periods. These buglers were subject to call for camp details. Each bugler, on reporting for duty to the regimental adjutant, would receive the orders for the various calls to be observed during the day as prescribed by the commanding officer.

The first call in the morning, usually about 5 A.M., was "Assembly of Buglers." The buglers would assemble at headquarters and in concert sound. "Reveille." This was the signal for the men to get out of bed and line up for roll call. About 15 minutes later, the

Recruiting for the Hawkins New York Zouaves.

buglers, again in concert, sounded "Assembly Call." Each company then formed in line in its own company street, and after being dressed by the first sergeant, the sergeant would call the roll. Each man was obliged to answer for himself, and, unless he had a legitimate excuse, his absence meant extra duty of some kind.

After roll call the sergeant made his daily report to his company commander of the number of men in camp, the number of sick (either in their quarters or in hospital), number present for duty, number on special detail, and the number AWOL. These reports were consolidated at regimental headquarters and then sent up through brigade, division, and corps, to army headquarters.

Immediately after roll call, the bugler at headquarters would sound "Stable Call." This call was not always uniformly observed. When a regiment was regularly encamped, each man took a nose-bag and marched with his company to the quartermaster's quarters, drew forage, and then proceeded to feed and curry his horse. In the field, each man tended to go his own individual way.

Battle of Big Bethel. Union Forces were repulsed with heavy losses despite a spirited charge by Duryee's Zouaves. (Fort Monroe Casement Museum)

Washington's birthday, celebrated by a ball at the 2nd Corps Headquarters. (From a sketch by Edwin Forbes)

Federal troops marching through the streets of Fernandina, Florida.

Chicago Zouave cadets. A group of Ellsworth's, organized in 1860.

A Union regiment countercharge to dislodge Rebels from farm buildings. Anyplace, sometime during the war.

The Grand Review of May 1865 in Washington,
D.C., when Johnny came marching home.

After the horses were fed and groomed, "Breakfast Call" was sounded, and the men then prepared their own breakfast. As long as a regiment was in regular quarters, company cooks usually prepared the meal for an entire company. Each man would take his plate and tin cup and receive from the company cook his allotted ration already cooked. But in the field this was not practicable and each man cooked for himself.

The next call was "Sick Call." In response to this call, those who were sick reported at the surgeon's quarters or hospital tent for prescriptions.

Then followed "Water Call." If the camp was near a stream, which was usually the case, this call was easy to observe; however, when it was necessary to take the horses a mile or more to water, it was a matter of no little concern.

The next call was "Fatigue Call." When in camp it was of the utmost importance to maintain the best possible sanitary conditions (as all students of the 1861-1865 period will agree, the conditions of many camps was anything but sanitary!). To clean the camp, a large number of men were detailed each day for fatigue duty, policing and

Veteran and the grandson playing soldier.

cleaning the streets, stable, mess-tents; burying refuse matter; getting wood and water for the cooks; and performing other necessary duties as they presented themselves.

After the men and horses were fed, the sick cared for, and the horses watered and groomed, the military duties of the day really commenced. They began with "Guard Mount." At the first call for "Guard Mount," the first sergeant of each company would report his detail to the adjutant. An inspection followed. While the details were marched up, the regimental band played marching music. The band also played during the inspection of the guard, and, at the proper time, would "sound off," exactly as at dress parade. The new officer of the day would then receive from the old officer of the day his orders. Then the new guard would be divided into three reliefs and would be marched back to the guard quarters.

The next call was "Drill Call." If weather permitted, the period from 9 to 12 A.M. was devoted to company drill. At noon, "Recall" was sounded, to be followed by "Dinner Call."

After the main meal, the bugle sounded "Assembly Call for Regimental Drill." At 2 P.M. the companies were marched out for drill, invariably directed by bugle notes. At 4 P.M. the headquarters bugler would sound "Assembly Call for Dress Parade"— the most imposing of all the military ceremonies. After this, there followed in close succession the evening calls: "Water Call"; "Stable Call"; "Supper Call"; and about 9 P.M., another "Roll Call."

There were several special calls, such as: "Officers' Call", "First Sergeants' Call", "Boots and Saddles", and "Taps." "Boots and Saddles" always created a stir and bustle in camp, especially when it meant the breaking of camp and going on a march or preparing to go into combat.

The soldier boy, in his great coat.

The funeral train bearing General Grant's body passing West Point.

"Taps" was the last call and was usually sounded at 10 P.M. It meant "lights out" when all, except those on duty, were supposed to be in bed.

Buglers in both cavalry and artillery units were usually close by their commanding officers. Naturally these buglers came under enemy fire and the records prove that many became casualties in the course of enemy action.

At the Battle of Front Royal, Virginia, September 21, 1864, Wilson's cavalry division, charging in a fog, was guided by the calls of 250 buglers, all blowing at the same time. Their combined blowing created "a swelling volume of sound," which might easily have frightened any force. Ten thousand men could not have made a greater noise and, since it came from all directions, the Confederates broke and ran in full flight. These 250 bugles are accounted for if one recalls that there were two at division headquarters, two at each brigade and regimental headquarters, and two with each battery or troop, and that Wilson had 10 regiments in his division—thus accounting for the 250 buglers present on this occasion.

7. Federal "Boy Musicians"

The minimum age for draft in the Federal Army was 18 years, but for some 40,000 eager boys in their early teens, an opportunity was presented by enlisting as drummers and fifers. And these youths were important; they sounded the calls for the everyday life of their fighting comrades, and even called them to battle.

Moreover, some 300 boys of 13 years of age or less (25 were 10 or under!) were actually accepted and enlisted.

Generally, this was as drummers or fifers, but, all the same, they were regularly enrolled and sworn in by the recruiting officer of the United States. The rub-a-dub-dub of the drums and the tootle-te-toot of the fifes inspired the Federal armies long after there remained in service but a few of the bands which marched to the front in 1861. All the calls from "Reveille" to "Taps" were rendered by the brave little boys who were as ready to go under fire as the stoutest hearted veteran. Many a time a boy would drop his drum or fife to grab up the gun of a wounded soldier and go in on the firing line.

In the 2nd Connecticut Heavy Artillery, Frederick D. Painter was the assumed name of one of eight or ten boys, not more than 13 or 15 years of age, who had enlisted and come to the regiment with the rest of the recruits, as drummer boys. Painter was killed by a shell at Cold Harbor while another young drummer of "G" Company was fatally wounded by a shell at Winchester.

Many stories have been told about bravery of drummer boys in the Civil War. A poem which was popular during the war centered around an incident at Vicksburg. In the disastrous assault of May 19, 1863, a boy came limping back from the firing line, stopped in front of General Sherman, while the blood formed a pool at his feet. Unmindful of his wound, he shouted: "Let our soldiers have some more cartridges, sir—caliber .54," and then trudged off to the rear. Another poem is based on an incident in the first year of the war, when a drummer boy had beaten his drum until he was struck in the ankle by a bullet. He refused to fall out, but, mounted on the shoulders of an older comrade, continued to beat his drum as his comrades advanced.

While at Louisville, Kentucky, a little boy arrived at the camp of the 75th Indiana Infantry. This young fellow gave a vivid account of two unsuccessful attempts to join the regiment as a drummer boy. His mother had prevented him joining the 19th Indiana Infantry at Camp Morton in 1861, but he had run away and followed the regiment's fortunes for three months in Virginia, when he was taken sick with typhoid fever, sent to a hospital in Washington and then returned to Indianapolis. In this city the 60th Indiana was guarding prisoners. The boy attempted to enlist in the regiment, but was turned down. But when the 60th Regiment left the state, the boy accompanied it as a cymbal player in the regimental band. Shortly after its arrival in Kentucky, almost all the regiment was captured at Munfordsville. The boy escaped and returned to Louisville. He then applied for admission to the 75th Regi-

ment into its first line of battle. He was with the 75th, carrying his drum at the head of the regiment, through all its marches and raids in Kentucky and Tennessee, until early in 1863 when he was forced to accept a medical discharge. "Andy" became Governor of North Dakota in 1892.

A young soldier of the 101st Pennsylvania Infantry has described what he saw as his

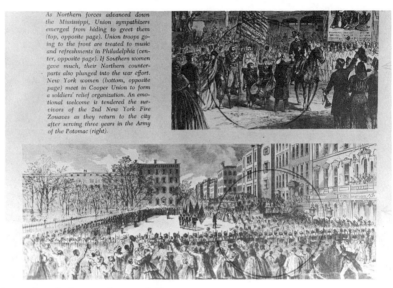

As Northern forces advanced down the Mississippi, Union sympathizers emerged from hiding to greet them (top, opposite page). Union troops going to the front are treated to music and refreshments in Philadelphia (center, opposite page). If Southern women gave much, their Northern counterparts also plunged into the war effort. New York women (bottom, opposite page) meet in Cooper Union to form a soldiers' relief organization. An emotional welcome is tendered the survivors of the 2nd New York Fire Zouaves as they return to the city after serving three years in the Army of the Potomac (right).

Emotional welcome is tendered the survivors of the 2nd New York Fire Zouaves as they return to the city after serving three years in the Army of the Potomac.

ment. A drum was brought out and the boy ordered to show his skill. He satisfied everyone that he was a good drummer and was mustered into the service as Albert Walton, a name he used to escape detection by anyone who might attempt to bring him back home. At the time of this enlistment he was 15 years old and by actual measurement was 4 feet 7 inces tall. He was the smallest member of the 75th! However, the youngest member was Andrew H. Burke, a drummer in "D" Company, who was only 12 years old at enlistment. "Andy" was a musician, who, on an eventful Sunday morning before daylight, at Lebanon, Kentucky, beat the "long roll" upon his drum, which called his regi-

outfit crossed into Virginia on March 1, 1862:

What a scene was spread before us! More than 100,000 troops were encamped within our view. The bray of one thousand mules, the neigh of cavalry and artillery horses, the sound of the bugles, the play of the drum and fife, and the music of the numerous brass bands, were doubly inspiring to us boys of Pennsylvania, whose ages ranged from sixteen to twenty years.

Some four weeks later, this regiment, as part of Casey's division, 15,000 strong, left for the front. It was escorted to Alexandria by the Marine Band. When the 150th Pennsylvania Infantry arrived in Washington its march up Pennsylvania Avenue was headed by a white-haired old man who had beaten a drum at Waterloo, ten little drummer boys, and several fifers, playing "Dixie."

James D. Lockwood, who served as drummer boy in a New York Heavy Artillery regi-

**Full dress, Ordnance, first sergeant. (From the
Smithsonian U.S. National Museum)**

102

Sergeant Major, full dress, Infantry. (From the Smithsonian U.S. National Museum)

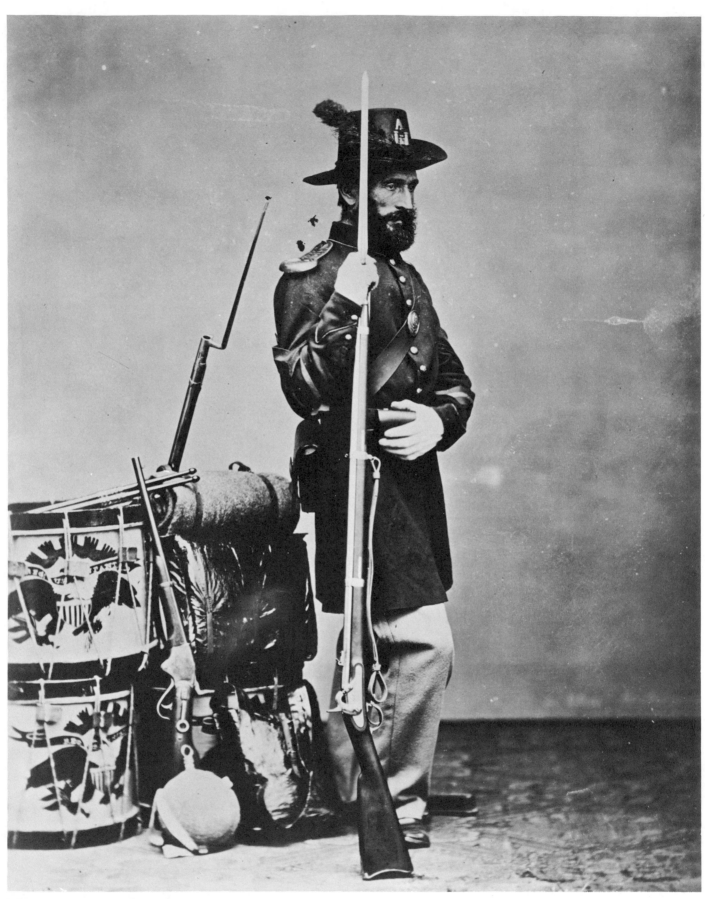

Soldiers' equipment. Ordnance sergeant with display of stacked muskets, infantry drums, a Spencer carbine, pistol, artillery saber, noncom's sword, cartridge boxes and belts, haversack, canteen, knapsack and blanket roll. (From the Smithsonian Institution)

**Cavalry musician, with Jeff Davis' hat and the
shoulder scales. Such finery was not in general use
after 1862 and many cavalry bugles were shorter
than the one show here. (From the Smithsonian
Institution)**

105

O. J. Lehman, Bethania, North Carolina, who organized and taught the band of the 33rd Regiment, N.C.S.T.

ment, enlisted at 13 years of age, and reenlisted as a "veteran" at the age of 15!

Musician Benjamin F. Fox, 96th Illinois Infantry, enlisted at age 14, was wounded in the right elbow at Kenesaw Mountain—was "always with the regimental band."

Charley King, drummer boy of the 49th Pennsylvania Infantry was 12 years 5 months and 9 days old, when he enlisted. He was shot through the body at Antietam, and died three days after the battle.

Clarence D. McKenzie, drummer boy of the 13th New York State Militia died in the service. At the time of his death he was 12 years old. He was killed by the accidental discharge of a musket in the hands of a comrade who was practicing the manual of arms. One of the young drummers of the 20th Illinois Infantry was killed; a small memorial volume about this youngster was even translated into German and published in Cincinnati during the war under the title *Der Klieine Tambour* (The Little Drummer).

Very probably the youngest drummer boy serving in the Federal Army was nine-year old Joseph H. White of Co. "A" 14th Connecticut Infantry.

Visitors thronged the camp of the 22nd

Wisconsin Regiment to listen to its band and watch little Johnnie Walker beat his drum. Johnnie, only 12 years old, was a favorite of the ladies who made much of the youngster, giving him such treats as apples, pies and cakes. When on the march this little fellow kept up the best he could with the big men, but when he got tired the colonel or some other officer would let him ride the officer's horse. Johnnie's mother sent him a suit of clothes, made exactly like an officer's uniform, while a lieutenant promised him a pair of shoulder straps with silver drum sticks on them.

A drummer boy of the 55th Illinois Infantry, Orion P. Howe, won the Medal of Honor for gallantry at Vicksburg. This boy, only 14 years old, while severely wounded and exposed to heavy enemy fire, refused to be evacuated to a field hospital until he had informed General Sherman of the urgent need for more cartridges for his regiment.

Probably the most famous of all Civil War drummer boys was little Johnny Clem, who at the age of 11 went to war with the 2nd Michigan Infantry. Not regularly enlisted, he accompanied the regiment to the front with his pay of $13.00 a month coming from the officers of his regiment. In the course of his combat career he came to be known as the "drummer boy of Shiloh and Chickamauga." At Shiloh his drum was smashed by

"The Rogue's March," unidentified.

GOING TO THE BALL

BALL ROOM.

THE SUPPER ROOM

THE GANDERS.

Parties, during the war.

Men entered the service, of all types, including some thieves, and if caught were dealt with harshly. Not only was he drummed out of camp at bayonet point but he had to wear a placard labelling him for all to see.

Fife and drum. The Regimental Corps. (From the National Archives)

Reveille on the line of battle and tattoo in camp, by Edwin Forbes. (From the Frick Art Reference Library, Union League Club, New York City)

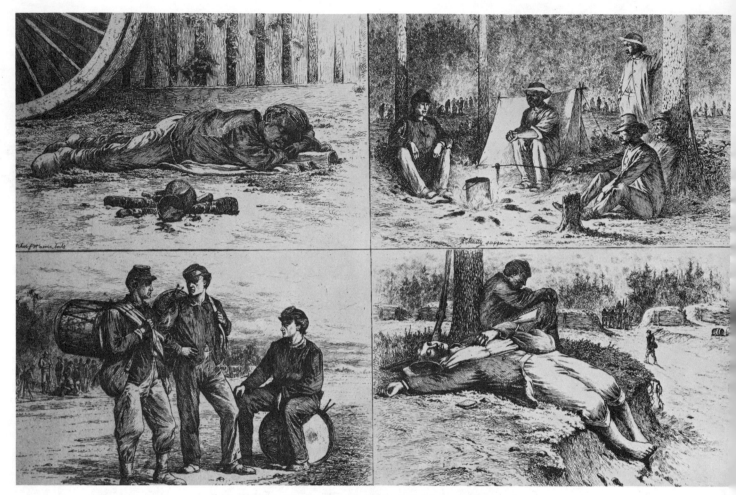

Four camp scenes which include drummer boys, by Edwin Forbes. (From the Frick Art Reference Library, Union League Club, New York City)

a shell; the incident (or a similar one) so impressed the writer of minstrel songs, Will S. Hayes, that he composed the famous song, "The Drummer Boy of Shiloh." There is doubt, however, that this song was inspired by Clem. At the advanced age of 12, little Johnny is reported to have shot a Confederate colonel out of the saddle during the Battle of Chickamauga. The youngster was twice wounded in battle, remained in the army after the war, and retired in 1916 as a major general.

These drummer boys were fated—because of their youthful ages at the time of their war service—to be among the last survivors of the War. In fact, the last survivor of the Grand Army of the Republic was a drummer boy, Albert Woolson, who served in the 1st Minnesota Heavy Artillery during the War.

In 1863 the United States Army *Regulations* decreed that:

The general superintendent [of recruit depots] will cause such of the recruits as are found to possess a natural talent for music, to be instructed (besides the drill of the soldier) on the fife, bugle, and drum, and other military instruments; the boys of twelve years of age, and upward, may under his direction, be enlisted for this purpose. But as recruits under eighteen

Appomattox station, at Lee's last attempt to provision his retreating army, April 8, 1865. A body of Federal troops captured the supplies.

years of age and under size must be discharged, if they are not capable of learning music, care should be taken to enlist those only who have a natural talent for music, and, if practicable, they should be taken on trial for some time before being enlisted.

The Acts of March 3rd and July 4, 1864, made it an offense to enlist any minor under the age of 16 years. Prior to the passage of these acts, a detachment of boys was kept under instruction at each of the regular army recruiting depots. These boys were not only carefully trained as young soldiers and musicians—*i.e.* drummers, fifers, and buglers —but were well taught in the common school branches of the post school. Many of the boys turned out to be good students and excellent soldiers, reaching as their age matured to the grades of non-commissioned and even of commissioned officers.

The duties of these youngsters were varied and exacting. For example; drummer boys of the 8th Maine Infantry were detailed to work with the surgeons at the amputating tables located at the field hospital. As one of them (George T. Ulmer, only 16 years old) later wrote:

It was a horrible task at first. My duty was to hold a sponge or "cone" of ether to the face of the soldier who was to be operated on, and to stand there and see the surgeons cut and saw legs and arms as if they were cutting up swine or sheep, was an ordeal I never wish to go through again. At intervals, when the pile became large, I was obliged to take a load of legs or arms and place them in a trench nearby for burial.

In addition to sounding the calls, evacuating the wounded, and occasionally carrying messages, drummer boys were often called

Grand parade, with the closing scene of May 1865 in Washington.

Snare drum. (From N.G.N.Y. Excelsior Regiment Company)

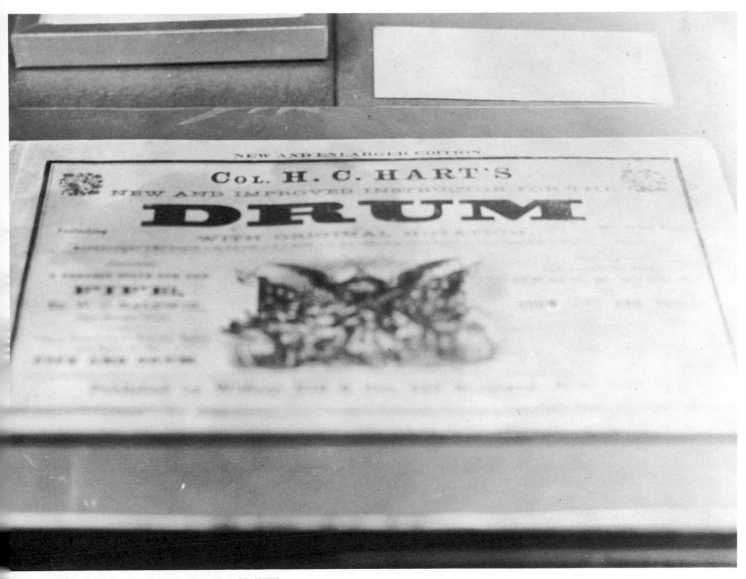

Drum instruction book, used during the Civil War by Colonel H.C. Hart. Fife and drum improved method.

Drummer boys of the 146th New York.

Band of the 97th New York. (From the book, Boys in Blue, Prospect Bros. Prospect, N. Y.)

On the parade ground. (From the Library of Congress)

Union troops. Parade and the crowds.

A parade on the drill field with the drum corps.

Regimental drum corps in close-up. (From the National Archives)

upon for various other duties. A drummer of the 104th Ohio Infantry, W. C. Richardson, served also as a barber, honed the surgeon's instruments and drew maps!

Some drummer boys had lots to learn about military life. George T. Ulmer of the 8th Maine Infantry, arriving at his camp for the first time, informed a sentry that he must see the colonel. The sentry, thinking the drummer boy had some important message, escorted him to the colonel's quarters. Ulmer woke up the colonel, told that august personage he was reporting, and wanted a bed. The colonel said, "Is that all you want? Corporal, put this man in the guard house." The Corporal did, and Ulmer was duly "put."

Of course there were exceptions to the tender age and appearance of drummers and fifers. In the 37th Iowa Infantry—known as the "Graybeard Regiment"—all men, from colonel down to drummer "boy" —were over the military age limit of 45 years.

Each morning the 13th Massachusetts Infantry was awakened by the veteran drummer "Dan Simpson" and "Si Smith," the fifer. "Old Si," as he was called, looked as though he was left over from the Crusades, so thin and worn with age did he appear. Both of these veterans had served in the War of 1812. At 5 A.M. they put in their appearance, and after some wrangling (since time had not improved their dispositions), they would sound the reveille which turned the regiment out for roll call. Smith weighed about 75 pounds but didn't look it. His coat sleeve, which seemed no larger around than a baby's arm, was covered with service stripes from wrist to shoulder. In spite of his thin frame, he managed to get wind enough to make his old fife sound clear as a bell. "Good Morning, Si" would be heard as the boys fell in for reveille, "How's your old friend, Miles Standish?"

8. Confederate "Boy Musicians"

Unfortunately, records on the "boy musicians" of the Confederacy are fragmentary. It is known that a large proportion of Southern boys in their teens enlisted in the Confederate service. However, the vast majority of them were enrolled in line units due to the need for all ablebodied soldiers in the ranks. Extensive research has uncovered a few examples of the Confederate "boy musician." One of these was Charles F. Mosby, a drummer boy, who enlisted at the age of 13 and served from 1861 to 1865 as a member of the 6th Virginia Infantry and later with Henderson's heavy artillery.

At the battle of Missionary Ridge, J. B. Thomas, a Confederate drummer boy, seized the musket of a fallen comrade, and shot down the color bearer of one of the charging Federal regiments. The flag fell, but a daring young Federal officer sprang forward and rescued it before the Confederate could take it away. The young officer was Arthur MacArthur, destined to attain the highest rank in the United States Army and to sire one of America's most famous soldiers — Douglas MacArthur.

A German, Jacob Gans, favorite bugler of Nathan B. Forrest, got three bullet holes in his bugle during one march to Pulaski, Mississippi.

A drummer of the 16th Mississippi Infantry, a notorious straggler, had lagged far behind his regiment when he saw a Federal cavalry unit approaching. He jumped into the woods and as the enemy drew near he commenced beating the "long roll." As this was the signal to form line of battle, the Federals, assuming that a Confederate force was hidden in the woods, turned their horses about and retreated. The drummer replaced his drum and continued his march as casually as before the interruption. The Confederates had a spy in the 114th Pennsylvania Infantry. This lad, only 13 or 14 years old, would stay for weeks at a time with the 114th, only to be absent for several weeks at a time. He was employed by Meade as a Confederate spy, but was finally caught. He then disappeared and the men of the 114th never saw him again.

A lone bugler can be partly seen at the peak of the loading platform sounding a call to the troops below.

Regiment forming for parade, a Guard Mount. (From the National Archives)

Infantry engaged at Rocky Face Ridge. The Second Minnesota, marched with Shermann to the sea, one of the finest fighting units in the Atlanta Campaign.

The Marines of the United States and Marine barracks at Washington.

Infantry parade, near Harper's Ferry, West Virginia. (A U.S. Signal Corps photo from Brady collection in the National Archives)

9. Problem of Morale: Pay, Discipline, and Punishments

Many regiments began under less than auspicious circumstances. Some of the men detailed to the drum corps of the 148th Pennsylvania Infantry were not musicians and others were not interested in serving in the corps. No opportunity was available for any kind of systematic drill. The complete lack of any knowledge of military drill was painfully apparent at the first guard mount. As the men assembled, it was at once apparent that a complete absence of uniformity in attire and equipment of the men was the order of the day. The colonel had several things to say, all unprintable. Some of the men had their arms with them, while others "didn't bother" to bring along their muskets. Some of the men were in shirt sleeves, others were attired in blouses, dress coats and even overcoats! The colonel turned his gentle admonitions on the drum major who appeared on this auspicious occasion in his shirt sleeves, without equipment of any kind, and topped out with a brilliantly variegated sleeping cap for a head gear!

Collis' Zouaves band, although small in numbers, was often selected over much larger bands to play at important functions at Army Headquarters. The bandmaster of this Zouave band believed that his men were preferred because of their style of music and their uniformly good deportment. The members of some bands often drank to excess, thus rendering themselves "disreputable" and "at the same time incompetent to perform their music in a proper manner."

The 20th Maine Infantry had a drum corps "in which every member drummed or fifed independently of all others." After some preliminary drilling of his regiments, the colonel decided to hold a dress parade. With much running around, the regiment was finally in line, the colonel in his place, when suddenly and prematurely, the drum corps broke loose and began to ramble down the line "uttering discords galore." Then followed the first order the colonel ever gave the regiment. The order was: "Captain Bangs, stop that damned drumming!" But neither Captain Bangs nor the drum corps heard the order. The colonel, as the noise continued, grew more and more wrathy, finally he charged upon that musical body with sword in hand. The musicians fled, disappearing around the nearest flank, and took refuge in the rear areas. The colonel

Zouaves on parade. (From the National Archives)

then turned his attention to an unmilitary looking lieutenant and ordered him to "draw up his bowels!" But the lieutenant was not able to improve his military posture and soon resigned and left the service.

Some bands were not too keen about soldiering. Although the band of the 2nd Minnesota Infantry contained some good musicians, the members were glad to receive their early discharge from the service and unceremoniously dumped their instruments in the woods before leaving for home. Later in the war, however, the regiment was better served by a new band, completely equipped with silver instruments financed by private subscriptions and the regimental fund.

Some bandsmen paid little attention to army regulations and were constantly in hot

Band in center. Confederates at Appomattox.

Drumming out Albany volunteers who refused to take the oath.

Recruiting for the Confederate Army at Woodstock, Virginia.

Execution of five deserters belonging to the 5th
Corps with General Sykes. (From the Library of
Congress)

Guard mount in the camp of the 1st Massachusetts.
Volunteers opposite the Rebel position. [This could
be Gilmore's band if from Twenty-fourth Massa-
chusetts] (From the Library of Congress)

March of the Grand Army, May 1865.

Lincoln. The last sitting on the day of Lee's surrender on April 9, 1865.

water with their military superiors. During the service of the band of the 22nd New York, the members committed "not a few" breaches of discipline; these musicians possessed a knowledge of military customs at the front in inverse proportion to their skill in music. The men apparently never could understand why they should not be out of camp after tattoo, nor why, if they were, they should not return by the shortest line, instead of going around by the guard tent. Neither could they be made to understand the object of the countersign or its use. Night after night the sentries would be heard calling "Halt! Who goes there?" and the reply, "I'sh de band."

It must not be assumed that all the young drummer boys were cute. Far from it! Some, by their own admission, were veritable demons. James D. Lockwood, drummer boy in the 4th New York Heavy Artillery, has left us with an example of his wares. Lockwood, walking by the "cook house" one day, saw the cook lying on a bench, fast asleep. The

drummer boy took a piece of tent rope and firmly tied the cook's leg to the pole which held the kettles containing the supper for the company. He then threw in the fire a handful of copper-cased pistol cartridges. Passing on down the company street, Lockwood saw a protuberance on one of the tents' sides. This was the head of a man who had just come off guard duty. The drummer boy could only see the bulge as an inviting target for a heavy stick he had picked up in the company street. The mighty blow drew blood from the sleeping soldier and some strong language, which in turn was followed by the cook's own expletives prompted as a result of Lockwood's previous misadventure. The cook was covered with ashes and grease and was lucky none of the live rounds had hit him, or any of the other men in the regimental camp area.

Poor bands often afforded the men opportunities for a good laugh. One of the poorer bands in the Army of the Potomac was to be found in the 16th Maine Infantry. On the day before Christmas 1863 the regiment received orders to move, although the weather was bitter cold. The cold was so sharp that in less than five minutes the band instruments froze up and the tune of "The Girl I Left Behind Me" quickly faded into silence. Christmas Day was spent in a marshy forest, bleak and dismal; "nothing 'merry' about it." The regiment was still stuck in the mud on New Year's Eve, but meanwhile the band had located some whiskey. The bugler sounded the call for muster, companies fell out onto the streets, but the band, which, should have assembled, was nowhere to be seen. The adjutant (who related this incident) finally found the Principal Musician and he inquired: "Mr. Shea, did you hear the call?" John Shea; always a gentleman, doffed his hat and managed to drawl slowly and politely "A'jtant, I hope you'll 'scuse me; I'm drunk."

A bugler of the 26th Michigan, player of taps. (Go to Sleep)

Veterans of the 6th Corps, Army of the Potomac, marching down Pennsylvania Avenue, Washington, D.C., June 8, 1865.

on "Traveller," September 1866. "I can only e is a Confederate gray."

Color Guard of the 8th Minnesota, with Sherman when Johnston surrendered on April 27, 1865 near Durham's Station, North Carolina.

General Blenker's Division. Torch-light procession in honor of the new commander-in-chief.

A bivouac fire on the Potomac.

Ambulances of the Union Army taking part in the Grand Review in 1865.

Crowds on June 8, 1865, while waiting the march of the 6th Corps of the Army of the Potomac. The pomp and panoply of war are here in the blare of trumpets.

"How's the B flat, Mr. Shea?"

"He's bad off's I am," was the reply.

"And how's the bass?"

"Dre'ful tired; slaying down."

"Are any of you sober?"

"Well, I'd say, A'jtant, we simply shouldn't play."

"Oh, nonsense! There's a cold spring of water down there. Send for a pailful or two, bathe your heads, and drink a quart of it, every one of you, and you'll be all right. Hurry up."

The adjutant returned to his quarters— soon came "Adjutant's Call"—the troops came to "Parade Rest." All right so far. But now the band was to march, playing, down to the front of the line and back again. With some misgiving the adjutant ordered "Troop —beat off." Away went the band, and the ground seemed very uneven under its feet; and now and then the leader would lose a note and, trying to catch it, would clash into the B flat; the bass drum persisted in coming down heavy on the up beat; the cymbals forgot to clang when they should, and closed with a crash when they shouldn't. The musicians, countermarching, started in quick time together; but somehow the orders of Mr. Shea were not quite understood, and half the band struck up one tune, the other half, another. This was too much. Above the discord was heard a loud and angry voice: "Parade is dismissed!" The adjutant received a reprimand, but the show was worth it. The men of the regiment soon burst out laughing and laughed so loud and

Parade, with the band up front as usual. Possibly in
New York City.

The army at rest, Company "K," Third Massachusetts heavy Artillery, in Fort Stevens, 1865.

Colonel John E. Bendix, German Regiment, "Steuben" volunteers receiving their flag at the City Hall, New York, May 24, 1861.

SONGS OF THE WAR DAYS

We leave our ploughs and workshops, our wives
  and children dear,
With hearts too full for utterance, with but a
  single tear;
We dare not look behind us, but steadfastly
  before:
We are coming, Father Abraham, three hundred
  thousand more!

Chorus—

We are coming, we are coming, our Union to
  restore:

division on the battlefield of Chickamauga. It is said to have
been sung by Captain Terry's regiment on the battlefield just
previous to the actual engagement.

The morning star is paling; the camp fires flicker
  low;
Our steeds are madly neighing; for the bugle bids
  us go:
So put the foot in stirrup and shake the bridle
  free,
For today the Texas Rangers must cross the
  Tennessee.

"FATHER ABRAHAM"

This photograph shows some of the members of the Twenty-second New York Infantry, who fought at the Second Battle of
Bull Run, Antietam, and Chancellorsville. It lost during service eleven officers and sixty-two men killed and mortally wounded
and one officer and twenty-eight enlisted men by disease. Notwithstanding, many of these men were among the first to enlist
again when Lincoln issued his call for 300,000 volunteers to fill the ranks of the army, a call that gave rise to the famous song of
that year, "We're Coming Father Abraham, Three Hundred Thousand Strong." Here they are at Harper's Ferry in '62 enjoying the luxury of a visit from a lady whose light gown is attractively spread out over her ample hoop-skirt at the right of the picture.
It is interesting to study the formal manner in which the men are holding their rifles, and also the grouping around the drum.

We are coming, Father Abraham, three hundred
  thousand more,
We are coming, Father Abraham, three hundred
  thousand more.

You have called us, and we're coming, by Richmond's bloody tide
To lay us down, for Freedom's sake, our brothers'
  bones beside;
Or from foul treason's savage grasp to wrench the
  murderous blade,
And in the face of foreign foes its fragments to
  parade.
Six hundred thousand loyal men and true have
  gone before:
We are coming, Father Abraham, three hundred
  thousand more!

SONG OF THE TEXAS RANGERS
MRS. J. D. YOUNG
AIR: The Yellow Rose of Texas.

This song was dedicated to Captain Dave Terry, a Texas
Ranger, who was conspicuous for bravery in General Wharton's

With Wharton for our leader, we'll chase the das-
  tard foe,
Till our horses bathe their fetlocks in the deep,
  blue Ohio.

'Tis joy to be a Ranger! to fight for dear South-
  land!
'Tis joy to follow Wharton, with his gallant,
  trusty band!
'Tis joy to see our Harrison plunge, like a meteor
  bright,
Into the thickest of the fray, and deal his deadly
  might.
O! who'd not be a Ranger and follow Wharton's
  cry!
And battle for his country, and, if needs be, die?

THE ALABAMA
WORDS BY E. KING   MUSIC BY F. W. RASIER

While the greater number of naval war songs belongs to the
North, crystallizing around the names of Farragut and Winslow
the heroism displayed by the small, scantily equipped Confederate
Navy, brought forth several lyrical tributes. This roysterin

Songs of the war days. Drummer boys were seen
everywhere. Photo of Twenty-second New York
Infantry, Harper's Ferry, 1862. "We're Coming
Father Abraham, 300,000 strong."

Jackson at Chancellorsville.

so long that the other regiments took it up; and so the good nature spread; and the adjutant was forgiven.

The band of the 6th Wisconsin Infantry was truly horrible; it could play only one selection—"The Village Quickstep." Its complete inefficiency could well have been due to its colonel's weird habit of assigning those men to the band who were musicians but rather the "eight-balls" whom he had decided to punish for infractions of army regulations.

Members of brigade bands also exhibited poor discipline. On January 1, 1863, it was ordered that all members of the 1st Brigade Band, stationed at Jefferson City, Missouri, who were found to be absent without leave, would be "arrested and placed in confinement until tomorrow when they will be placed upon a train and sent to headquarters of the district."

The following examples, taken from the files of the National Archives, are indicative of the ever-present problem of poor discipline in the Federal bands.

Damon Morse, musician in the Engineer Brigade Band on November 21, 1863, went on parade intoxicated and unfit for duty. He was also charged that day as being AWOL.

John Ryan, musician of the band stationed at

Fort Monroe, Virginia, stole a watch and chain, April 13, 1864.

On January 27, 1864, Charles Bellosa, musician in band of 1st Brigade, 1st Division, 6th Corps — "drunk on duty"

Franz Kramer, musician, "conduct prejudicial to good order and military discipline (drunk)."

Generally, the band had its own special area for its members. In each regimental camp there were also several tents or, in the early weeks of soldiering, about ten barracks placed in a row. Sometimes there would be a small building in the middle of this row of buildings for the regimental band before July-August 1862, when these bands were sent home After this, the new organizations—brigade bands—were found in tents near brigade headquarters.

Regulations for pay were specific. By General Order No. 48, July 31, 1861, it was stated that:

The bands of the regiments of infantry will be paid as follows: One-fourth of each will receive the pay and allowances of sergeants of engineer soldiers; one-fourth, those of corporals of engineer soldiers, and the remaining half, those of privates of engineer soldiers of the first class. The drum major or leader of the band was to receive the pay and emoluments of a second lieutenant of infantry.

In 1863, "Field Music" monthly pay was as follows:

Principal musician	$21.00
Chief Bugler or Trumpeter	$21.00
Bugler or trumpeter	$13.00
Musician	$12.00

At the same time, members of Brigade Bands were paid as follows:

Leader	$45.00
Four members (each)	$34.00
Eight members (each)	$17.00
Four members (each)	$20.00

Pay of buglers and musicians was raised on May 1, 1864, as follows:

Chief bugler, cavalry	$23.00
Bugler, cavalry	$16.00
Principal musician, infantry	$22.00
Principal musician, artillery	$22.00
Leader, regimental or brigade band	$75.00
Musician	$16.00

Because of the ambiguity of the original 1863 order, it was decreed by General Order No. 231, July 18, 1864, that members of regimental and brigade bands were to be paid as heretofore, i.e.—one-fourth of the members of each band $34.00 per month; one-fourth of them $20.00 per month; and the remaining half of them, $17.00 per month.

Discipline in some drum corps (as, for example, the Corn Exchange Regiment), was very lax in 1863. The duties of many of the musicians consisted mainly of drawing rations and eating them. But when the 1864 campaign began, a reformation took place; General Barlow introduced a system to utilize the wasted energy of the "sheep-skin batteries" as they were often called, by consolidating all the musicians of the division (1st Division, 2nd Corps) into one body. General Barlow placed a mounted lieutenant in command with a sergeant detailed from one of the companies, in charge of the musicians of each of the four brigades. Since there was an average of four regiments in each brigade, there were 16 regiments in the division. This meant that the division contained 16 drum corps of about ten boys in each, or about 160 musicians in the division. All musicians who had lost or thrown away their instruments (as some frequently did during a summer's campaign) were sent to their companies and placed in the ranks as privates. The others were marched in a body in the rear of the division and immediately on the opening of an engagement were put to work erecting hospital tents under the direction of the surgeons. Details were made and sent to the front to bring the wounded to the field hospitals. Many were detailed as nurses and others kept continually at hand for any emergency that might occur.

Much friction occurred between the sergeants of Barlow's division and the young musicians of the various drum corps. This was partly due to the "disinclination" of

The men of the 74th New York Infantry, in which a band and drum corps are clearly seen. Stationed at Camp Scott on Staten Island, N.Y. until August 20, 1861, then moved to Washington after the Federal defeat at Bull Run.

Union regiments. Many started the war with complete and magnificent bands. One photo shows a band in Arlington, Virginia; next appears the 164th New York; next the post musicians of Fortress Monroe wtih their bearskins; and the last, a band at Camp Stoneman near Washington.

Grand Review, probably early in the war. At ast two or more bands can clearly be seen with eir over the shoulder instruments. (Thomas Nast, tist)

137

Galusha Pennypacker, Colonel of the 97th Regiment.

Joshua T. Owens, Colonel
of the 69th Regiment.

James A. Beaver, Colonel
of the 148th Regiment.

Isaac J. Wistar, Originally
Colonel of the 71st Reg't.

Joshua V. Siegfried, Originally Colonel of the 48th Regiment.

FEDERAL GENERALS

No. 23

PENNSYLVANIA

David H. Williams, Originally Colonel of the 82d Infantry.

John B. McIntosh, Origi-
nally Colonel of the 3d
Cavalry.

Frederick S. Sturnbaugh,
Originally Colonel of
the 2d Infantry.

Thomas J. McKean Led
a Division at
Corinth.

Montgomery C. Meigs,
Quartermaster-General
of the Army.

Federal generals of Pennsylvania.

New York troops at Washington, by General
Sandford, in presence of the President and Cabinet,
July 4, 1861.

the boys to submit to discipline and partly to the "assumption of authority" by the sergeants. Severe punishments were rare, but occasionally they did occur. One such incident resulted from the capture of five musicians by the provost guard. The boys had captured a Confederate calf and appropriated it for their own use, since rations had been short. Taken to division headquarters, the five youngsters were "bucked and gagged." All the musicians of the division assembled to witness the penalty imposed by General Barlow. Six strokes on the shoulders with an ox "gad" as they sat in their cramped and helpless position, were given each, and as the last stroke fell, the tall form of the general crowded through the outer circle and asked "Who administered those blows?" The executioner saluted and replied: "I did, General."

"Well, Sergeant," retorted the General, "You may report to your company; I will not have a Sergeant in my provost guard who does not obey orders. Those blows were not nearly so heavy, nor the stick so large as I ordered." The main "crime" of the boys was that they had been caught. Foraging was common. The mode of punishment was humiliating to the soldiers and should have

been beneath the dignity of a general in the army.

One case of insubordination took place at Falmouth in the early spring of 1863. A very muddy wagon road ran directly through the center of the camp of the "Corn Exchange Regiment." One dark and disagreeable night the drum major wanted "tattoo" beaten on one side of the road, but other members of the drum corps wanted to play on the side where their quarters were. Both factions mustered numerous musicians. The result was what might have been expected of two divisions of a musical organization, thirty feet apart and trying to play so complicated a piece as "tattoo" at the same time. Before the piece was half way through, the stentorian voice of the colonel was heard. "If you don't stop that infernal racket, I'll put you all in the guard house."

The rank of musician in the army was often considered trivial and somewhat degrading; so much so, that, some were loath to accept it, if allowed their own choice.

Many musical organizations had their "characters." One such was an eccentric Frenchman belonging to a divisional headquarters band of the 2nd Corps. During a "grand review" of the Army of the Potomac

Entering Richmond. The Federal troops, April 3rd, 1865, their reception on main street. (Sketch by Joe Becker)

Appomattox Court House, with soldier and citizen. Grant left soon after the surrender for Washington.

Ninety-sixth Pennsylvania Infantry at Camp Northumberland, near Washington. (From the Brady Collection, Library of Congress)

Musician, full dress, 1861 light artillery.

Ruins in Richmond. Federal soldiers tramp past the blazing ruins. (Sketch by Becker)

A wedding in the Army of the Potomac, with drums being used as an altar.

Musicians were punished for foraging as were the other soldiers. A musician of Co. "H", 106th Pennsylvania Infantry, was convicted of stealing a turkey from a farmer. He was compelled to pay for the turkey, and was then taken to the guard house and compelled to march up and down in front of the guard house, under guard, for two days with the turkey tied to his back. Ever after this incident, the musician was called "Turkey." At first he was disposed to fight back, but found he could not prevail, and ever after swallowed his mortification.

at Stevensburg, Virginia, Abraham Lincoln was the guest of honor. As was customary, the musicians of the entire division formed at the head of the column, then later fell out and faced the reviewing officer, while the entire division passed. In the maneuvering to face the President, the Frenchman, playing a slide trombone, ran his slide through the head of a drum, to the "chagrin and amusement" of the other bandsmen. The appearance of this man was likened by a comrade to one of Shakespeare's witches dancing around the boiling cauldron.

Entering Richmond with the Union Army, April 3, 1865.

10. Band Uniforms

FEDERAL BAND UNIFORMS

In general, bandsmen wore the uniform of the regiment or branch of service to which they were assigned. According to United States Army Regulations (Section No. 1663), the commanding officer could, at the expense of the unit, and sanctioned by the Council of Administration, "make such additions in ornaments as he may judge proper." The 1863 Regulations, Section 1484, prescribed uniforms as follows:

For all musicians—the same as for other enlisted men of their respective corps, with the addition of a facing of lace three-eighths of an inch wide on the front of the coat or jacket, made in the following manner: bars of three-eighths of an inch worsted lace placed on a line with each button six and one-half inches wide at the bottom, and thence gradually expanding upward to the last button, counting from the waist up, and contracting from thence to the bottom of the collar, where it will be six and one-half inches wide, with a strip of the same lace following the bars at their outer extremity—the whole presenting something of what is called the herringbone form; the color of the lace facing to correspond with the color of the trimming of the corps.

Naturally, there were many variations in wearing of the uniform. Roland Barrows of the 18th Massachusetts Infantry band wrote to his sister on December 19, 1861, that their uniforms were much too small, especially the jackets. Each member of this band was given a nightcap, white knitted material, gathered at the top in a little tassle!

According to a musician of the 18th Massachusetts Infantry band, writing home on April 8, 1862, near Yorktown, Virginia, all the bands in the service were carrying their knapsacks. The bandsmen of the 18th, however, left all their other luggage, including the Zouave uniforms back in Georgetown in storage. The men didn't want anything with them more than they could comfortably carry on their backs. As the 18th Massachusetts musician said: "When I can't carry my knapsack, I shan't go myself."

Later, however, even the knapsacks were left behind. By late May 1862, bandsmen of the 18th Massachusetts were carrying very little "impedimenta" but were being called on to furnish music from time to time. In fact their horns were so badly used up on these marches that the regimental officers were forced either to replace them with new instruments or dispense with the band altogether.

CONFEDERATE BAND UNIFORMS

Confederate Army regulations specified

Review of Confederate troops en route to Virginia as they pass the Pulaski Monument in Savannah, Georgia, August 7, 1861.

RECRUITING IN THE PARK

Recruiting in the park. A drum was used to attract attention.

Union troops going to the front are treated to music and refreshments in Philadelphia, Pennsylvania.

Reception of General M. Corcoran by the major and citizens of New York City, August 22, 1862, on his release from Confederate prison in which he had been confined for one year.

Seventy-first New York sailing for war. Well known for its stirring marches of the band. The Jackson Light Infantry served as part of the Dan Sickles' Excelsior Brigade.

**Marine Corps band. A battalion at the Washington
Navy Yard, April 1864.**

The Post band, of Fort Monroe, Virginia, December 1864. (A Brady photo from the Library of Congress)

a double-breasted tunic of gray cloth, trousers of light (or sky) blue, double-breasted cadet overcoat with cape, French-style caps, black leather tie, and Jefferson-style boots "according to pattern." However, the average Confederate soldier or bandsman was never outfitted in anything like regulation-style. Probably one of the best uniformed bands was that of the men from Salem, North Carolina, serving in the 26th North Carolina Infantry. They wore "cadet jeans, with brass buttons."

11. Band Instruments

Actual designation of individuals' instruments is rarely found. One of the very few is given in the history of the 72nd New York Infantry of the "Excelsior Brigade." The nucleus for this regiment's band was the Jamestown Cornet Band which furnished eight musicians, soon joined by other bandsmen from Dunkirk and Fredonia. A complete band was organized in August 1861 as follows:

Leader, A. G. Peters	1st B Flat Soprano
Director, W. B. Norris	1st E Flat Soprano
F. P. Boynton	2nd E Flat Soprano
A. H. Tew	3rd E Flat Soprano
J. S. Lathrop	4th E Flat Soprano
H. K. Willard	2nd B Flat Soprano
D. C. Smith	3rd B Flat Soprano
C. H. Warren	1st E Flat Tenor
J. W. Wheeler	2nd E Flat Tenor
A. N. Ayres	3rd E Flat Tenor
R. H. Dickenson	4th E Flat Tenor
J. H. Blackney	1st B Flat Tenor
M. F. Curtis	2nd B Flat Tenor
T. H. B. Chase	Baritone
E. M. Barclay	1st B Flat Bass
C. Curtis	2nd B Flat Base
H. G. Bailey	1st E Flat Tuba
L. L. Akin	2nd E Flat Tuba
A. M. Comstock	Side drum
Wm. Sandford	Side drum
W. H. Gibson	Bass drum
D. C. Dinnin	Cymbals
M. F. Tower	Asst. Bass Drum

This was one of the many bands mustered out in the fall of 1862.

The 1st Massachusetts Cavalry had a band of 31 members equipped with the following instruments:

Bass drum	3	E Cornet	4
Snare drum	2	B Cornet	2
Cymbals	1	Cornet	1
B Bass	1	Alto	6
B Tenor	6	Tuba	3
E Clarinet	1	Key Bugle	1

The supplying of instruments to bands varied greatly from time to time and from unit to unit. According to Section 969 of the 1863 United States Army Regulations:

Regiments will be furnished with field music on the requisition of their commanders, made, from time to time, direct on the general superintendent [of the depot] and, when requested by regimental commanders, the superintendents will endeavor to have suitable men selected from the recruits or enlisted, for the regimental bands.

Musicians in the 11th New York Cavalry band had to furnish their own instruments. Their leader, a competent band director in civilian life, was commissioned a second lieutenant and instructed to enlist competent musicians. He was so successful that the band became one of the best in the service. But later the regiment was scattered at various posts in the Department of the Gulf, and sickness and death reduced the band in members. In July 1864, the lieutenant resigned his commission and when he left he took his instrument and all the music with him. The mustering officer refused to discharge the men from the service, but without a leader, leading instrument, or music, the band was of little use and the men returned to their companies. Subsequently the band was reorganized; instruments and music were provided through money raised by the officers. In later years band members were sorry to see that some men of the regiment thought that the band had a "soft snap." Actually, members of the band believed they were faithfully performing the duty for which they had enlisted and they insisted in later years that they did not have a "picnic" all the time as some men in the regiment had always supposed.

Silver cornet instruments were purchased,

One Hundred Fourteenth Pennsylvania. Soldiers of Company "F," at Petersburg, Virginia, August 1864. (From the Library of Congress)

Rebel troops arriving at, and departing from Martinsburg, Virginia.

Drum and bugle. (Virginia sketches by special artists)

Recruiting of colored troops, and the drummer boy. Come and join us brothers. (From the Chicago Historical Society)

A group of soldiers, undated and unidentified. (Photo from the Chicago Historical Society)

at considerable expense, for ·the band of the 48th Ohio Infantry.

After the battle of New Burne the 27th Massachusetts Infantry found some "weather-beaten" cornets, bearing the names of "Toman and Russell, Boston," hanging from some trees. The Confederates had left these instruments in their hasty flight. The discovery of these instruments, plus the fact that the 27th was willing to get rid of them, was the genesis of the decision of the 44th Massachusetts Infantry to start its own band.

On January 3, 1865, the leader of the 3rd Brigade Band asked and received permission for the band to receive 20 days leave to return to Massachusetts to get their instruments repaired, to get new music, and to recruit more musicians.

Drums were carried by a broad strap of webbing slung around the neck. Brass hold-

Seventh New York Cavalry, camp scene. (From the National Archives)

Band, unidentified. (From the National Archives)

154

Band of the 4th Michigan Infantry. (From the National Archives)

Sixty-seventh New York Infantry, camp. (From the National Archives)

ers for the drum sticks were items of issue, but, often as not, the drummers stuck their drum sticks inside their belts. Another item of issue was the long, straight "musician's sword," which was very effective in tripping up its wearer. Its main value was as use for a spit when some hapless chicken came within the eager scrutiny of the ever-ravenous drummer boy!

According to Section 113 of the 1863 United States Army Regulations:

The front of the drums will be painted with the Arms of the United States, on a blue field for the infantry, and on a red field for the artillery. The letter of the company and number of the regiment, under the Arms, in a scroll.

Drums were put to many uses. They were often used to sit on or as a field desk in active campaigning. A unique use of drums was contributed by men of the 14th New Hampshire Infantry. One evening at dress parade, the colonel became incensed at the absence of several of his drummers. Just before he left the parade ground, three of the delinquents were observed coming into camp. Perceiving that they were observed, they put on a bold front, and passed quite near their commanding officer. Obsequiously saluting, the spokesman remarked, sotto voce, "Colonel, we have got some fine pork in our drums here: shall we leave a nice piece at your tent?" The colonel replied in a rather loud and severe tone: "If you are sick, report yourself to the surgeon; don't come around here troubling me!"

Some of that pork was placed where it would do the most good.

Cymbals were definitely used in some Civil War bands. In the history of the 39th Illinois Infantry a photograph of its band taken in 1864 shows cymbals. This band is of unusual interest in that the leader received the pay of a second lieutenant, which was made up by a tax on the sutler!

Under the new order concerning bands, each brigade was allowed one brass band, but the regiments were compelled to confine themselves to the snare drum and fife.

Many colonels did not fully understand the limitations of the instruments of their "field music" units. While guarding a railroad in Maryland, at a regimental drill, the colonel of the 148th Pennsylvania Infantry stationed his drum corps in a nearby grove and asked the bass drummer to beat time. The day was very stormy and the colonel, not making allowance for the poor acoustics due to the rain, threatened destruction to the drum and the drummer himself. The drummer's friends were actually afraid the colonel was going to run his sword through the hapless drummer.

MAKERS OF MUSICAL INSTRUMENTS

(The following list, while not complete, contains positively identified makers of instruments during the Civil War Period.)

Baker, John A., New York

Sixty-seventh New York Infantry, camp. (From the National Archives)

New York 7th was famous for its spit and polish uniforms early in the war.

County Court House. (From the Michigan Historical Society)

Beal, Wm., Lowell, Mass. (drums)

Blanchard, Porter, Concord, N. H., (bass and tenor drums, fifes, drum sticks, repairs)

Blume, Fred, New York (musical instruments and the "Excelsior Music-book," containing patriotic songs)

Byrne, George C., N. Y.

Eisenbrant, Philadelphia (a large fife has his name on it)

Firth, Pond & Co., New York

Getron & Abbott, New York

Godwin, Jos. H., New York

Hall, Wm. & Son, New York (1861 contract for drums, musical instruments, bugles, cocoa wood fifes)

Hartley, Wm. B., New York

Hitchcock, H. H., New York

Joerdens, J. F. M., Snare drums

Horstman Brothers & Co., New York and Philadelphia (cavalry bugles)

Laflin, Walter, New York

Meacham & Co., Albany, N. Y. (maple wood fifes 17 inches long, brass ends)

Mein, Richard, Drums

Merrill, L. T., New York

Pepper, J. W. & Son, Philadelphia (his name is on a horn)

Philips, Andrew J., New York

Rogers, Alexander, Infantry drums.

Schmidt, H., Williamsburg (military drums)

Smith, James J. A., Batavia, N. Y.

Smith, J. T. & Co., New York

Stratton, John F., New York (his name is on a horn. Also, cavalry bugles have been found marked Stratton & Foote. A military drum bearing Stratton's name is marked "Military Band Instruments, Maiden Lane, N.Y. 1860." The drum is maple with a five-point star in front)

Zoebisher, C. A. & Son, New York

General Steven's brigade taking possession of Beaufort, South Carolina, on the evening of December 5, 1861.

Gillmore's headquarters, showing a "Rush Hawkins" in 1863, wearing the one foreign uniform retained throughout the war.

Mourning. Honor the brave picture to Soverign Brown by artist George H. Durfee made in 1863. The drummer was a 14 year old boy who died in Alexandria in 1862, probably from wounds received at Fredericksburg.

Battle of Gettysburg, showing Longstreet's attack left center, Blue Ridge in the distance.

Citizens of Baltimore barricading the streets, Monday evening, June 29, 1863. (From a sketch by Edwin Forbes)

Civil War drummer boy from a Zouave Regiment
is a bit of decoupage. (Abby Aldrich Rockefeller
Folk Art Collection at Williamsburg, Virginia)

Lincoln at Gettysburg, November 1863, dedicating
the National Cemetery.

12. Life in Camp

Duties of bands in camp, while not especially arduous, were often exhausting. A bandsman of the 11th New Hampshire Infantry tells us that he could endure more manual labor than "the very exhausting labor of horn-blowing." When in camp, the bandsmen were expected to play at "Guard Mount," and then practice at least four hours daily, concluding with music at "Dress Parade" at 5 p.m. The 11th New Hampshire, while at City Point, even had its bandsmen erect many of the log buildings used there during the winter of 1864-1865.

Of course, many bands were used for entertainment of soldiers and civilians alike. Early in 1863, Gilmore gave a series of concerts for the benefit of Massachusetts regiments in the Department of North Carolina. Among the list of subscribers were some of the most affluent Boston merchants. The various military associations, such as the New England Guards Association, Tigers, Cadets, and Lancers, took a warm interest in the success of these concerts. One company contributed a grand piano, which yielded $1,691. The total receipts were $5,772.65.

In the 18th Connecticut, the band often gave a concert after mail had been distributed to the men. For example, on September 30, 1862, an observer wrote as follows:

Perhaps we don't have any music in this camp. Step in among us some night and see if we don't . . . From Capt. Bates' company's street, away out there on the left, a blended harmony, produced by the upper part of the street singing 'Rock of Ages,' while the lower half are 'putting in' with "Wait for the Wagons," floats over me; next on their right, Lt. Mathewson's company are singing "John's Brown's Body," by snatches, and "There'll be no sorrow there," with energy. Capt. Bowen's boys add to the volume the touching strains of "Old Dog Tray" . . . The street in front of me (company C) swells the chorus with three or four different kinds of music, including one-Jews-harp and three fifes . . . [mixed in] is an occasional howl of a dog.

But often the weather was too cold for the brass band to play. On January 5, 1862, Roland Barrows of the 18th Massachusetts Infantry band wrote home that the weather had been so cold that the band had not been able to play for three days, and the drummers had been taking their place.

Occasionally, music in camp worked to the disadvantage of the immediate audience of such entertainment. In the last hours before the surprise attack of the Confederates on Grant at Shiloh, Beauregard heard Federal bands playing marching songs throughout most of the night. To Beaure-

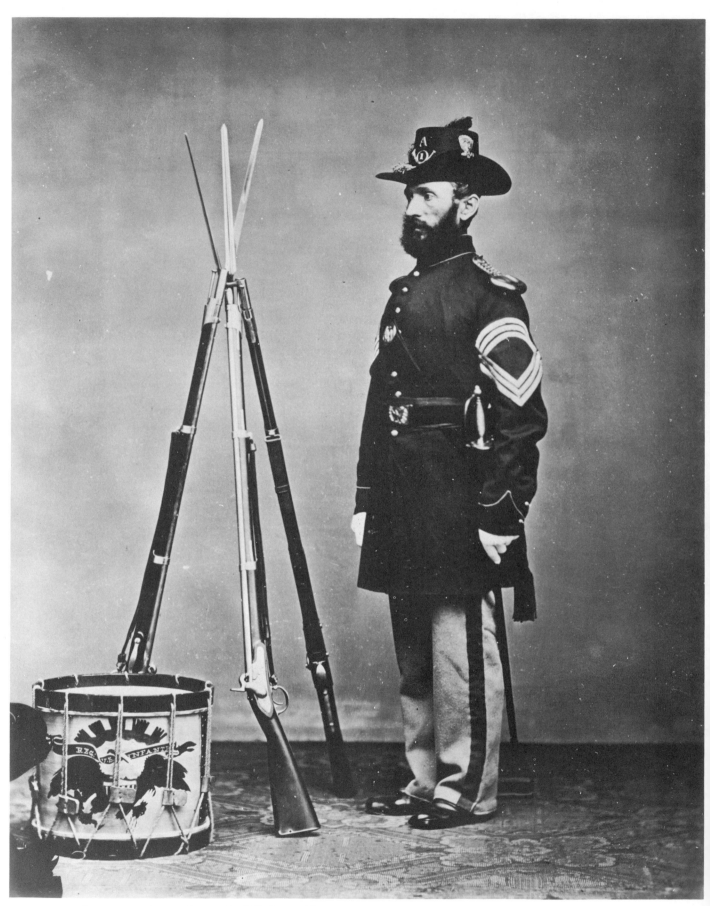

Sergeant major, Infantry in full dress. (From the
Smithsonian U.S. National Museum)

Musician, full dress, Cavalry. (From the Smithsonian U.S. National Museum)

"Music in Camp." Union soldiers in the just deserted Confederate camp at Fredericksburg on May 3, 1863, in which the camera has caught a dramatic moment.

Various forms of entertainment around the campfire, like the Negro fiddler.

Talented young volunteers under the Southern Cross, in the first year of the war. The musicians are betrayed by the violin and bugle.

Charge of Duryee's Zouaves. Attack by the 5th Regiment of New York volunteers at the Battle of Great Bethel.

At Bull Run, Union forces at 2:00 P.M., July 21, 1861.

gard, this could only mean that Buell had come up and the Federal forces, intrenched, were now so numerically superior to the Confederates that the attack should be called off. Beauregard was in error: Buell had not come up. Moreover, the Federals were unaware of the close proximity of the entire Confederate army.

A common service, albeit unpleasant, was the drumming out of service of deserters from their units. The deserters' heads were shaved after which they were marched up and down the company streets or about a square formed by their brigade. This marching was done under guard; the musicians' role was that of playing the "Rogue's March."

A deserter from the 63rd Pennsylvania Infantry had the buttons cut off his uniform, his head shaved, and was branded on the hips. He was then drummed out of camp. On his back a board was hung, inscribed with the word "Deserter." Eight men lined up in back of him with fixed bayonets. In

Julia Ward Howe in 1861. The author of the magnificent "Battle Hymn of the Republic," she was born in New York in 1819. She died at Newport, October 17, 1910.

The "Battle Hymn of the Republic," "A Hundred circling camps."

Drummer boys of the 2nd Fire Zouaves, New York, a parade and leave taking.

Parade on Memorial day and a reunion a number of years after the conflict.

this case, the music was furnished by a band, although often only drummers and fifers "drummed" a man out of the service. As the deserter from the 63rd Pennsylvania was escorted from camp, hundreds of spectators gave him a "parting salute" by throwing old shoes, tin pans, and other items at the unfortunate man. He was turned loose to go where he saw fit, forever disgraced. Feeling his disgrace deeply, he never returned to his home, and his fellow soldiers and civilian friends back home never heard of him again.

Sometimes only drummers were used to drum men out of the service. For example, on June 29, 1861, a member of the 7th Illinois Infantry, sentenced by Court Martial to be "drummed out of the regiment," passed through two lines of men, accompanied by two drummers who kept up a "terribly discordant drumming," while the men kept up a hooting and hissing.

In more serious cases bandsmen were used to furnish music at executions. When two men from the 74th Illinois Infantry were "shot to death by musketry" their entrance to the place of execution was led by a brass band, playing a death march. After the execution, the band played the spectators off the field with a "merry tune" which was designed to take some of the weight from the men's hearts."

Civil War musicians were kept very busy both in camp and at the front, playing dirges at the funerals of their comrades who fell victim to disease or enemy bullets.

PARADES

The dress parade was the culminating military spectacle. To many it was "the poetry of tactics, the mathematical perfection of soldierly display." The dress parade was the most critical test of military efficiency and thorough drill; it was the finest example of the accuracy of tactical training and the unity of a military organization. For those in command it was a practical inspection; and for all, field and line officers, rank and file, it was, when properly con-

The Civil War soldier as he really looked and marched. Twenty-second New York drummer boys. Attitudes are as prosaic as uniforms are picturesque.

ducted, a fitting close to the military day in camp.

There were elements outside the regiment which had to be essentially correct if the parade was to be a success. The parade ground itself could not be "sandwiched between cramped and disagreeable environments." A pack of stray dogs and half a dozen wooly-headed urchins were not spectators of an inspiring sort. Nor could an ideal parade be formed on the finest square or park of a great city with thousands of observers crowding the color-line, pressing the flanks, and generally obstructing the formation and the view.

There was a fascination in every stage of the parade, from the first note of preparation to the closing tableaux. The drummers first beat the musician's call, then the assembly on the color line, and the stereotyped warning of the first sergeant: "Company 'A', fall in for dress parade." Then there were brought forth the white gloves and brightened brasses of accouterments; boots were polished; and the soldier came from his tent cleaned up and respectable in appearance for half an hour in the day, if no more. There was always some laggard who could not find his musket or belt or some other item of equipment. Then followed the inevitable dispute for position on the left. It took the entire war to convince some volunteers that somebody must stand at the foot of the line and in the rear rank. From each company then came the "one, two, one, two" of the "count twos," the growling bass and piping falsetto, together with the comic emphasis of some odd genius, varying the monotony of the proceeding. With a "present arms!" the first sergeant received the captain, surrendered his temporary importance, and stepped into the ranks. There was no better occasion for sizing up the company commanders than the few minutes elapsing between the adjutant's call at dress parade and the call to form on the colors. In each company street the company commander and his lieutenants appeared before their men in full dress. Some officers, while waiting for the signal, would browbeat their companies, to pay off a score or two with some private or non-com.

Drum in the center. The charge of the 1st Iowa
regiment with General Lyon at its head, at the
battle of Wilson's creek, near Springfield, Missouri,
August 10, 1861.

Drummer boy, drumming up a charge.

"Yankee Doodle," good to fiddle, dance or sing, and
just the thing for fighting.

Federals enter Vicksburg triumphantly on July 4, 1863.

Some would put their companies through a rapid execution of the manual of arms, while in some companies, the officers were well balanced, dignified, and, while maintaining the proper reserve, won over their men by a kindly, genuine interest in their welfare.

But all were thrilled as the band struck up on the right, and the colors with their guard, marched to the line of parade; the spectacle was sufficiently stirring to move the dullest observer. It was usually just before sunset, the music was both martial and patriotic. Two or three other regiments in the brigade would also be in line for the evening dress parade; the near and distant drum corps; the far-off bugle call of some cavalry squadron; the rumbling of a light battery galloping into camp from an afternoon's target practice; while on the regimental parade ground the companies were being put through some preliminary drill—all this enlivened and made brilliant the occasion.

A good adjutant and sergeant major always made a noticeable impression on dress parade. Veterans never forgot the shrill

Lincoln.

Band photo of the 8th Elmira New York State Militia, Arlington. (A Brady photo from the Library of Congress)

tenor commands, "Attention, battalion!"; "Prepare to open ranks!"; "To the rear—open order—march!" The surpassing charm of the dress parades lay in the brass bands and the drum corps. Many regiments were proud of their bands. Many were not first class musical organizations, but they were the best the men knew. As a veteran of the 14th New Hamphire Infantry wrote in later years:

We were fond of the burly, whole-souled leader; and we became attached to the physiognomy of every member. Yes, the high private who tailed the bass drum, and boasted (when away) that he played in the band; his ramrod erectness and solemn tread—became a cherished feature of dress parade.

The entire regiment heartily enjoyed the slow-time music of the band passing down the front, and the quick measures of the return march. The parade formed, the drill in the manual, the marshalling of the first sergeants to report, the march of the line officers to receive the colonel's instruction, the dismissal of the parade, and the eager marching into camp, breaking ranks, throw-

ing off of equipments, and falling into line for rations—these incidents, following each other in a panorama most impressive to the young soldier, came to mind vividly after the lapse of years.

SERENADING

Bands were often called on to serenade "the brass" or popular regimental, brigade, division, and corps commanders. For example, on January 31, 1863, the band of the 14th Connecticut Infantry, probably the best in the 2nd Corps, went to Army Headquarters and serenaded the new commander, "Fighting Joe" Hooker. Another Connecticut regimental band (the 2nd) shortly before Bull Run, serenaded the colonel and then each captain of the regiment. The band ended with "Bully for That" a tune much in vogue at the time.

Serenading could be overdone. For example, during the Gettysburg campaign (June 20, 1863), the band of Collis' Zouaves serenaded General Birney in the morning;

Band of the 107th, U.S. Colored Infantry. (A Brady photo)

General Buford's engagement with Stuart's Confederate Cavalry at Boonsboro, Maryland, July 9, 1863.

Third Connecticut Infantry, Camp Douglas.

Army of General Hooker on the march to Chancellorsville. (Sketch by Edwin Forbes)

in the afternoon General Humphrey; and in the evening General Graham.

While stationed in Annapolis, the band of the 114th Pennsylvania Infantry (Collis' Zouaves) escorted exchanged Federal prisoners of war to Camp Parole. Sometimes there would be several thousand of these survivors of Confederate prisons at one time, ragged and emaciated. But in spite of their condition they fell promptly in line, and as soon as the band struck up, would march in good order to their camp.

Some regiments, without bands, were often assisted by bands from neighboring regiments when serenading the colonel was called for, or as a send-off on the march. For example, when the 39th Massachusetts Infantry (a unit without a band) broke camp at Poolesville, Maryland, on April 11, 1863, the ever-obliging band of the 14th New Hampshire Infantry turned out in the driving rain to give them a hearty send-off. It was a nice gesture, very timely too, as an awful march followed for the 39th with mud and water up to their knees.

While passing through Raleigh, North Carolina, a staff officer of General Atkins'

staff (as described in the history of the 92nd Illinois Infantry) requested permission for the band to serenade what he thought to be a "Female Seminary." The General, with a wink to his other staff members, gave the requested permission. Away went the staff officer with the band, and "soon music was floating out on the air" but the ladies, making signs with their fingers, soon revealed to the staff officer that his music was unheeded and unappreciated by the deaf mutes he was serenading!

BANDS IN HOSPITALS

At the vast military hospitals in the North, everything possible was done for the sick and wounded. The West Philadelphia General Hospital of 2,860 beds, had quarters for surgeons, attendants, nurses, guards, musicians, cooks, printers and other essential personnel. A good military band under "Professor" Theodore Hermann provided daily concerts and music for the dress parades as well as dirges for the dead.

Even more like modern hospitals was Mower General Hospital, also in Philadelphia. This installation of 4,000 beds, had an Administration and Medical Department which occupied a two-story building in the

McClellan's body guard.

178

Camp Curtin, near Harrisburg, Pennsylvania. A rendezvous of the Pennsylvania volunteers. (Sketched by Jasper Green, Esq.)

Manassas Gap Railroad and the Alexandria and Warrington Turnpike, at White Plains. Arrival of reinforcements for Beauregard at camp of the Tiger Zouaves. (From Harper's September 29, 1861)

The Charleston Zouaves.

James river canal, a view near Balcony Falls. Rebel troops going from Lynchburg to Buchanan on their way to West Virginia. (From Harper's September 28, 1861)

Orchestral lancers a la Verdi.

Organ-ized guard of grinders.

a Verdi stockade

Grand charge of Tromboniers

The Maestro conducting a siege in person.

Musical artillery-firing a 40 crochetter.

Music for the time. (From Harper's Weekly May 4, 1861)

center of the hospital. At the far corners of the hospital grounds were barracks for the guards. A large commissary building faced the railroad. Kitchens, dining halls, power and heating plants and various other structures were grouped in the open space in the center of the hospital wards. A roomy parade ground and a band stand were also in this central area. A full band and a drum corps furnished music daily.

ON THE MARCH

Bands were used to lead the line units out of bivouac when a forward movement was ordered. The music of the band was a great boon to weary men on a march. Illustrative of this was the reaction of the 11th Ohio Battery and other Federal units after the Battle of Corinth. The men were pressing closely on a retreating enemy but on the second night's forced march the men could only stumble along, almost dead with fatigue. Suddenly a band struck up the familiar song "John Brown's Body," other bands joined in, and soon the men were awake and swinging along without a thought of their weariness.

Many of the slaves had never heard a brass band and when Federal bands passed through their areas these slaves became wild with excitement and love of the music.

The 170th New York on reserve duty. A soldier
group in a moment fit for song.

For miles they would accompany the marching columns, dancing, jumping, and yelling with delight.

General Birney, of the Army of the Potomac, on entering a town would halt his division until the band could take a position on the corners of two prominent streets. He then would have the band play until the entire division had passed those corners. This impressed the towns' citizenry but the band then had to "double time" to get to its place at the head of the column.

Bands were very much in evidence during the Gettysburg campaign. At an early hour on Wednesday, July 1, 1863, the Federals began to march to Gettysburg, the 1st Corps in the advance, followed by the 11th Corps. Among these troops was the famous Iron Brigade, including the 6th Wisconsin Infantry. In this magnificent regiment—counting only 340 officers and men—the men were in the highest spirits. As they advanced to meet the confident Army of Northern Virginia, the Wisconsin regiment unfurled

The bodies of the 6th Massachusetts soldiers killed at Baltimore received by the citizens of Lowell.

Recruiting for the Confederate Army in Woodstock, Virginia.

their colors and marched through Gettysburg behind their drum corps. The colonel of the 83rd Pennsylvania Infantry told his men to unfurl the regimental colors and to have the march accompanied "by the sound of the ear-piercing fife and spirit-stirring drum." The drum corps struck up the "old national air" of "Yankee Doodle" . . . The enthusiasm was contagious. In a few moments it had spread from regiment to regiment, and from brigade to brigade, until every banner was flying, every fife screaming, and every drum beating.

13. At the Front

MUSIC IN BATTLE

Civilians in the early weeks of the war believed that the position of the band in parades—that is, at the head of the marching column, would also be the position in battle. Hence, enlistment in the band gave special opportunity for distinction in the field. The common thought was the outgrowth of observing the drum major and his bandsmen at the fore-front in parades and drills and the bravest men were generally supposed to be those placed in front. But battles were not fought in that order of formation, and bands never lead bayonet charges with music. There were occasions when bands, functioning as music makers, were in considerable danger however. In an entry of October 11, 1864, the 18th Pennsylvania Cavalry's historian noted: "We always have the band playing on the front in an advance, and tooting defiantly in the rear on retreat."

The first occasion when bandsmen came under fire was April 19, 1861, when the 6th Massachusetts Regiment fought the mob on its march through Baltimore. When they arrived in Baltimore, the band, being unarmed, refused to leave the railroad station. Eventually, however, the bandsmen left the railroad cars but were promptly attacked by the mob. The band members fought back the best they could, but soon their attackers were crawling under the cars and others were forcing their way in. The band fled leaving music, instruments, clothing, and equipment behind. On their way out they saw squads of police who were very obviously regarding the whole affair as a big joke. They told the band members to "run like the devil," which they did! The police refused to do any more than attempt to take care of the property left behind. After running about half a mile, the band met a group of Irish, German, and American civilians who took them to their homes, removed insignia from their uniforms, and substituted old clothes as a disguise. The 6th Regiment band members were treated as well as if these civilians had been blood relatives; everything possible was done to help them escape the mob, and any attempt to repay was regarded as an insult. Eventually, under the protection of 400 Baltimore policemen, these unarmed musicians were able to reach the cross-town railroad station and take a train back to Philadelphia.

Other regiments profited from the experience of the 6th Massachusetts: When the 7th New York left for the front, the bandsmen carried revolvers to protect themselves against the Baltimore mob. And when

"Come and join us brothers." Lithograph in full color published by the Supervisory committee for recruiting colored regiments. (From the Chicago Historical Society)

Zouaves passing Independence Hall, from Philadelphia in the Civil War.

The 6th Vermont Infantry before Camp Griffin, near Washington in 1861.

The bugler, a charcoal sketch.

New York State Militia, drum corps, Arlington, Virginia, June 1861. (From the Library of Congress)

the 1st New Hampshire marched through Baltimore, May 27, 1861, Fife Major F. H. Pike, "knowing that he was supported by a thousand loaded muskets beat right and left with his baton, clearing the way before him while Baldwin's Cornet Band played . . . Yankee Doodle in the first national air that had greeted the ears of the people since the passage of the Massachusetts 6th . . . It was amusing to watch the annoyance it occasioned in a large portion of the spectators."

During McClellan's Peninsular Campaign several bands saw actual combat. Among these was the band of the 10th Massachusetts Infantry. This band came under heavy fire at Fair Oaks where the bandsmen were stationed directly in rear of their regiments. While waiting for casualties to evacuate they came under artillery fire from both sides—Albert Ingraham received an ugly wound in the shoulder from a shell fragment which passed through his body and out near the backbone. During a brief lull in the fighting, a 14 year old drummer boy of this regiment was using his blackened cup to fill his canteen from a spring. McClellan rode up, asked for a drink, which of course, he

got. The lad apologized profusely for the battered condition of the cup, but Little Mac made one of his ready friendly replies and left an ardent admirer behind as he rode away.

At Williamsburg some Federals began to beat a hasty retreat at a critical moment in the battle. General Heintzelman, seeing his men running to the rear, drew his sword, waved it above his head, crying out with his peculiar nasal twang, "Halt! Halt! you — — —! Halt!" At this moment some members of a band came up. On seeing them, the General shouted, "Halt there! Halt! Give us Yankee Doodle or some other—doodle!" The band struck up a national air (not Yankee Doodle)—it produced the desired effect.

One of the many casualties of McClellan's campaign was Drum Major Marshall S. Pike, 22nd Massachusetts Infantry band, who was unfortunate enough to be a prisoner in the hands of the enemy when his band was mustered out in the Fall of 1862.

On the Peninsula in 1862, the 104th Pennsylvania Infantry, in retreat, had lost all its camp equipment except the regiment's

Drum corps. (From the Library of Congress)

Parade and inspection. (From the Library of Congress)

Buckley's minstrels. A songsheet of the times, deposited September 26, 1863.

Music on the homefront. (The breakdown from American Home Scenes)

whiskey ration which had not yet been issued. As a cook of one of the companies "was thought to be over-fond of the beverage," a drummer boy was left in camp to watch it. Soon, enemy bullets began to whistle through the camp, and the cook beat a hasty retreat. The drummer boy soon followed, since the whiskey needed no further watching, as a bullet had pierced the bucket and all the precious stuff was wasted on the grass. That same day, one of the regiment's drummer boys was reported for fighting and, as punishment, he was tied to a tree, but was soon released in order to go into action with his regiment. Another drummer seized a stray musket and used it throughout the entire day. This took place at Fair Oaks, first in the series of the bloody battles for Richmond. A few days later after incessant rain, the regiment was struggling to advance through nearly impassable muddy roads. The men came to a stream, and waist deep, officers and men waded through. The current took some off their feet, carrying them several yards downstream. Accordingly, a squadron of the 8th Pennsylvania Cavalry formed a line across the stream further down to prevent the infantry from being washed away altogether. The drummer boys, too small to wade, were carried across the roaring stream on the officers' horses.

Post musicians, of Fortress Monroe with their bearskins. (From the Library of Congress)

Campaigning took its toll—among both line units and their musicians. A former commander of the famous 55th New York Infantry, composed of men of French extraction, noted the depleted ranks of his regiment after a few months' campaigning:

What a contrast between the departure and the return! We had started out in the spring, gay, smart, well provided with everything. The drums beat, the bugles sounded, the flag with its folds of immaculate silk glistened in the sunshine. And we were returning before the autumn, sad, weary, covered with mud, with uniforms in rags. Now the drummers carried their cracked drums on their backs, the buglers were bent over and silent; the flag, riddled by the balls, torn by shrapnel, discolored by the rain, hung sadly upon the staff, without cover.

Well could the commander ask where his men were. We could have answered "Killed at Williamsburg, killed at Fair Oaks, killed

Service by Reverend Weston, Chaplain of the 7th Regiment at Camp Cameron on Sunday May 5, 1861.

Fall of Richmond. Victorious Federal troops tramp down main street of the gutted Confederate Capital on April 3, 1865.

Charge of Duryee's Zouaves. 5th Regiment of New York Volunteers at the battle of Great Bethel.

at Glendale, killed at Malvern Hill, wounded or sick in the hospitals, prisoners of Richmond, deserters, we knew not where."

At South Mountain, September 14, 1862, the band of the 45th Pennsylvania Infantry went into action at the head of the regiment. It played "Rally Round the Flag, Boys" as it moved up the mountain "opposite the corn field on the left." At that point the band was ordered out of the line by General Reno who was killed shortly afterward.

Three days later, at Antietam, some Federal bands actually accompanied troops into action.

The Confederate general, John B. Gordon, tells of a Federal charge at Antietam, where a band was used to inspire the men in their attack. This attack, launched in a massed formation, consisted of four lines of battle. Cheered on by the band in their rear and led by their commander on horseback, "this magnificent array moved to the charge, every step keeping time to the tap of the deep-sounding drum." Naturally, the result was never in doubt. Waiting until the Federals were almost close enough to see the button designs, the Confederates fired with such appalling effect that "the entire front line, with few exceptions, went down in the consuming blast."

At Fredericksburg, December 13, 1862, the band of the 14th Connecticut Infantry struck up "Dixie" but a staff officer stopped the playing because of danger from enemy fire. However, the band of the 10th New York Cavalry accompanied General Bayard across the river and played in front of General Franklin's headquarters on the night of December 12, 1862. The next morning the band was under a heavy fire, and General Bayard ordered them to go back to the river. They did so, but later returned to watch the fighting and General Bayard ordered them back a second time. This was the General's last order; he was killed before the return of the orderly by whom he had sent the message.

It was the 10th New York Cavalry band which furnished the music at Todd's Tavern, Virginia, May 7, 1864, for which credit has so often been awarded to Custer's band. The 10th Band became badly broken up by the capture and wounding of several of its members at the time of the Trevillian Station engagement. As a result, it accepted replacements from other regiments to en-

York, Pennsylvania. Scott occupied by Pennsylvania and Ohio Volunteers. (Sketch by Jasper Green)

Drums to the left, maybe near Chancellorsville. (From the Library of Congress)

able it to continue functioning as "the best band in the whole Cavalry Corps."

As the Confederates shelled the Federal position at Fredericksburg, a Federal general decided to draw this fire away from his troops. Accordingly he and staff took position on a hill where they could be easily seen by the Confederate artillerists. The move was very decidedly a success; the general and his staff were soon the target of many guns. The distance was consider-

able, however, and no damage was done except for spattering men and horses with mud thrown up by the projectiles. Just at this moment some members of a band of a new nine-months' regiment, whose colonel had ordered "the music" to remain behind while the fighting men moved up, happened to stroll up the top of the hill, attracted by curiosity to see what was going on. The bandsman whose business it was to beat

Second Rhode Island Infantry at Camp Brightwood near Washington. (A Brady photo from the Library of Congress)

First U.S. Veteran Volunteer Infantry Band, probably the grand parade on May 23, 1865. (From the Library of Congress)

the big bass-drum set it deliberately down and began to look over the exciting scene—including the river, wreathed in the smoke of a hundred guns, the city beneath, torn by bursting shells, the plain and heights beyond, bristling with entrenchments. Completely green, this genial recruit had no idea that, at such a distance, he could be in any danger, until suddenly the fire of a battery was turned upon the staff officers,

close by. Several projectiles in his immediate environment suddenly clarified the situation for the recruit, who, with ludicrous haste, ensconced himself behind his drum, where, though the drum walls would not have shed even a pistol bullet, he cuddled up with an apparent feeling of relief and security, which, fortunately was not disturbed by the impact of a three-inch shot.

The band of Collis' Zouaves numbered

Band of the 10th Veteran Reserve Corps, Washington, D.C., April 1865. (A Brady photo from the Library of Congress)

only 15 pieces, but was constantly being complimented for the excellence of its music. While crossing the Potomac River, it was heard by Secretary of State, Seward, who complimented the regiment's officers on the good music of their band.

Attached to this regiment was a vivandiere (Marie), who assisted the band members in caring for the wounded during battle. While thus occupied during the Battle of Fredericksburg, the entire band was captured by Confederate skirmishers.

Their instruments were taken from them and, after a short tour in Libby Prison, the men were exchanged. On their return, to the regiment, they were presented with a full set of superior instruments, donated by friends at home, as an acknowledgment of their gallantry and good service.

At Chancellorsville, Hancock, seeing the ever-increasing extent of the disaster resulting from Jackson's surprise attack, ordered every band and drum corps to play "Rally Round the Flag" and this took place while

Confederate uniforms.

these bands were being shelled in their positions. During the pandemonium caused by the fleeing 11th Corps, the attempt to resist it by the Federal troops, and the movements of the attacking Confederates, the band of the 14th Connecticut Infantry, the best in the Army of the Potomac, performed heroically. This band went directly into the open space between the Federals and the advancing enemy, with shot and shell crash-ing all about them, and played "The Star Spangled Banner," "The Red, White and Blue," and "Yankee Doodle" and repeated them for fully twenty minutes. They never played better. Did that require nerve? It was undoubtedly the first and only band concert ever given under such conditions . . . Its effect upon the men was magical . . . [although none of the band was killed, probably one or two were wounded] and one or

Market place at Winchester. Rendezvous of the Rebel Militia of the valley of the Shenandoah, with several drum corps.

Gilbert J. Marbury, Co. "H" 22nd New York Infantry. Photographed by the trail of a Napoleon field piece near Harpers Ferry in 1862. (From the National Archives)

Bull Run, showing the Rebels bayoneting wounded on the battlefield.

Drum corps, No. One corner Church and Car Streets, West Chester, Pennsylvania. (Photo by E. Woodward)

Fife and drum corps. Regimental field music, when a unit reached the front the musicians generally ceased to function as such and acted as litter bearers in evacuating the wounded. At other times their music helped keep up the morale of the men in the ranks. (From the National Archives)

Miamisburg, Ohio, Henry Shuey in center, fourth from left, further identified as a brother of Captain Harrison M. Shuey. (Lloyd Gatendorf of Dayton, Ohio)

Headquarters, General Hays, from collection of Lloyd Ostendorf, and drummer boy age 13, Pennsylvania Volunteers, 1861. (Photo by Brady at Fort McHenry, Maryland)

two of their instruments were marked with scars from that scene."

At Gettysburg, when every man was needed on the firing line, musicians of some regiments seized muskets and fought in the ranks.

On the Weldon Railroad in late 1864, General Hancock placed one of his bands in a sheltered position and ordered it to play patriotic airs to inspire the fatique details constructing a defense line. The Confederates fired a shell which went over these "dispensers of harmony" and the music stopped as though it had been cut off with a knife. A shout of derision arose from both lines.

On November 15, 1864, while the city of Atlanta was in flames, the 33rd Massachusetts Infantry band played "John Brown's Body."

At Dinwiddie Court House, just before Lee's surrender, advanced elements of Grant's army, consisting mainly of cavalry (with a few pieces of artillery), found themselves confronted by superior enemy forces. Sheridan, sensing the situation at once, had all the bands in his command commence playing and to continue playing until further orders. One band tried "Hail Columbia," another played "Lanigan's Ball," while a third came out with "Johnny Fill up the Bowl" and "Yankee Doodle." But these selections were not as monotonous as one faithful band, with never a stop, repeated "Hail to the Chief" until the nearness of the attacking Confederates and the wounding of the "E flat" warned the musicians to retire. While observers noted that the quality of this music was not up to the highest professional standards, they did comment enthusiastically on the good effect on morale. "The music animated and inspired the troops," while it doubtlessly awed the enemy.

Sheridan even ordered his bands onto horseback to charge with the line units. This was in the last days of resistance just before Lee's surrender.

As Grant and Sheridan rode forward toward Appomattox to receive Lee's surrender, a Federal band near the town was heard playing "Auld Lang Syne."

At Five Forks, Virginia, in sight of skirmishers, one of Sheridan's bands, mounted on gray horses, played "Nellie Bly."

Among the first troops to enter Richmond on April 3, 1865, was the 13th New Hampshire Infantry leading the entering Federal column, with their drum corps playing "Yankee Doodle."

Horace Porter tells of finding one of Sheridan's bands at Five Forks playing "Nellie Bly" as cheerfully as if furnishing music for a country picnic. Sheridan made the most effective use of his bands. They were usually mounted on gray horses, and instead of being relegated to the usual duty of carrying off the wounded and assisting the surgeons, they were brought to the front and made to play the liveliest airs in their repertoire, which produced excellent results in sprucing up the spirits of the line units. After several of their instruments were pierced by bullets, and the drums crushed by shells, as often happened, the music tended to be somewhat less than spontaneous!

TRUCES

One of the remarkable phenomenons of the war, unique in any war and any period of history, was the amazing lack of animosity between the combatants during lulls in the fighting. A striking illustration of this occurred during the winter after the blood bath at Fredericksburg. The two armies, totalling some 150,000 men, confronted each other across the Rappahannock in plain view and sound of each other. One evening massed Federal bands began a concert of

**Funeral of Colonel A.S. Vosburg, on May 21, 1861,
one of the first army officers to die in the war, was
held in Washington. (Drawing by A.R. Waud)**

popular songs and such Northern favorites as "Tramp, Tramp, Tramp," "John's Brown's Body," and "The Battle Cry of Freedom." The thousands of Blue and Grey soldiers listened through one piece after another until finally the Grey soldiers called on the Federal bands for some Southern music. The Federal musicians at once responded with "Maryland, My Maryland," "The Bonnie Blue Flag," and of course "Dixie." As a finale, the bands played a non-partisan piece —"Home, Sweet Home." And only a few weeks later these same boys were killing each other by the thousands at Chancellorsville!

During the many informal armistices, the pickets were friendly and exchanged newspapers as well as food for Southern tobacco. Occasionally, a band on one side would play patriotic airs and, after a while, their opponents would ask to hear their own patriotic tunes. Usually these requests would be rendered. Often, the band concert would end on a neutral theme.

A soldier of the 12th Georgia Infantry told of a time when in the midst of the protracted struggle at Spotsylvania, both sides had removed their wounded and were enjoying a brief respite from the severe fighting. A Confederate band moved to an elevated position of the line and played "Nearer My God To Thee." The last note of this beautiful hymn had just ended when a Federal band played the "Dead March." This was followed by the Confederate band with "The Bonnie Blue Flag." As the last notes died away, a great rebel yell went up. The Federals then played "The Star Spangled Banner." From the responsive yell which greeted this selection it seemed as if every man in the Army of the Potomac had been listening. The Confederate band then played "Home, Sweet Home," and a united yell went up from the men on both sides— "such a one as was never heard among the hills of Spotsylvania County before or since."

MUSICIANS AS STRETCHER BEARERS

During combat, musicians were generally sent to the field hospitals where they assisted the surgeons at the operating tables or went to the front with stretchers to bring off the wounded.

The band of the 13th New Hampshire Infantry had a very hard night's work after the bloody afternoon of Fredericksburg, December 13, 1862. The bandsmen took stretchers and followed their regiment in the charge on the Confederate position. The musicians kept only a few paces to the rear. After returning from the charge, the bandsmen hastily removed the wounded; they even went up to within a few yards of the enemy's front line, where they were continually fired upon.

Soon after organization, in the fall of 1861, the 20th Massachusetts Infantry began ambulance drills from 10 to 11 A.M.

each day. These drills involved the 24-member band plus a detail of one man from each company. There were five ambulances and one twin-horse spring wagon used. The band members were taught to compress an artery, apply a tourniquet (or make one from a handkerchief if a regular one was not available), to put on bandages, and to carry men in litters to the waiting ambulances.

Musicians of the 148th Pennsylvania Infantry were detailed to carry stretchers to the wheat field at Gettysburg on July 2nd. The following day was spent in assisting at the amputating table and securing straw to lay the wounded on. Wounded were constantly evacuated. On one of their trips the stretcher bearers were removing a wounded man to the rear, partly out of danger (but still under shell fire). During a brief halt to rest they were amazed to see the "wounded" soldier get off the stretcher and flee.

General Hancock was a great believer in military music. He instructed the drum corps of the Corn Exchange Regiment in what was expected when high ranking officers appeared, ending with the advice: "Play some appropriate music, such as 'Hail to the Chief.'"

J. B. Holloway, a drummer of Company "D" 148th Pennsylvania Infantry, has left a graphic description of the duties of a musician in battle. Holloway and his fellow musicians were organized into units, under lieutenants and sergeants, for the purpose of caring for the wounded. During the most bloody campaign of the war—from the Wilderness through Petersburg—Holloway was on detail to assist at one of the operating tables. His unit was responsible for putting up and taking down the hospital tents, arranging the tables for operations, providing a plentiful supply of water, cleaning the operating instruments, holding the limbs during amputation, and burying those same amputated limbs afterwards. The men

The cigar box violin by Edwin Forbes. (From the Library of Congress)

would dig a hole near the hospital tent and fill it up with severed arms and legs. When the hole was full, it was covered up and another promptly dug. More than one lawn or yard in front of a Southerner's palatial residence did Holloway and his fellow musicians convert into a burying place for the limbs of Federal soldiers. Holloway also served as a stretcher bearer at Gettysburg where he saw Colonel Cross of the 5th New Hampshire mortally wounded. Cross' sufferings were so great that he begged for someone to shoot him. He died before another

dawn could illuminate the carnage of the fight.

The young musicians were to witness much improvised surgery. A musician of the 148th Pennsylvania Infantry on duty with a stretcher unit saw a man who had been shot through the throat. The wound was so deep that his throat was swelling shut. As the soldier writhed in agony, a surgeon went to him, laid him on the ground, ran an instrument into his throat and windpipe, and inserted a silver tube. The soldier was relieved of his suffering

Drum corps in camp. Union soldiers. (From the Library of Congress)

temporarily only to die shortly afterward.

The musicians had their work cut for them during the great battles of 1864, especially at the Wilderness, Spotsylvania, and Cold Harbor, where the losses were frightful. The bandsmen developed a system for taking care of the wounded. Those wounded who were unable to care for themselves were placed on the ground in rows side by side and row after row, with space enough between the rows so that the musicians could get through to supply their wants—and the one overwhelming request was for water. These human rows were usually formed in the woods close to roads leading back from the firing line. The more severely wounded were put in tents when tents were available. From these field hospitals the wounded were sent in ambulances and army wagons to the nearest boat landing or railroad point, and from there shipped North. When an army wagon was used, the men were placed in a sitting posture with their backs to the sides of the wagon box, alternating from side to side until the wagon was full. Then the end gate would be put in and "away they would go through the mud and over corduroy roads."

Drummer J. B. Holloway of the 148th Pennsylvania Infantry described his activities in the Wilderness where he was charged with the care of the 20-25 wounded men in tents. Among these was a soldier who had been shot centrally through the forehead, the ball coming out at the back of the head, and the brains oozing from both bullet holes. This man, quite strong, and delirious, kept wiping the brains from his forehead. He continually tried to get up and the drummer spent the entire night holding him down until finally relieved the next morning. Whether the wounded man survived or not is unknown. As this drummer recorded after the war: no one could place his finger on any part of the human body but what the drummer could truthfully say: "I saw a man wounded there." The largest flesh wound this drummer saw was a man at the Battle of Totopotomy Creek. This man was shot through the buttocks with a shell or some large missile, and the flesh was laid open as if someone had plowed a furrow through it. A person's two hands would not have covered the wound.

Some medical officers have left recorded appreciation of the services of bandsmen in removing the wounded. Surgeon Edward P. Roche has related how the band members from the 56th Massachusetts Infantry evacuated wounded across a river which had been greatly swollen by a thunder storm. The river had to be crossed because any delay meant certain capture for wounded and well alike. No bridge was standing. The surgeon gathered the band members and explained

Drummer boys of the war days, identified by comrades half a century later.

Charles F. Mosby, One of the boy drummer soldiers, a Confederate. He enlisted at the age of 13 and served from 1861 to 1865. First with the "Elliott Grays" of the 6th Virginia and later with Henderson's heavy artillery.

**Union drummer boy at Beverky Ford, Virginia,
August 11, 1863. (By Edwin Forbes, Aug. 1863,
from the Library of Congress)**

the situation. First, the men threw the guns and equipment into the river and then attempted to get the wounded across the river by carrying them on their backs, two men wading and swimming with each wounded man. But the attempt so exhausted and chilled the men it was abandoned. A raft was made from the flooring of an old mill nearby, capable of holding three men at a time. No ropes could be found to pull the raft, and the only means of propulsion was for the men to strip off their clothing and swim and wade the river, pushing the raft ahead of them. It took six men most of the time to make the trip and they were up to their necks in water almost all the time. The danger and work involved in transporting 50 wounded men in this fashion entitled these bandsmen to great credit. They toiled all through the night and into the next day; these men were a credit to their state and their regiment. Many other army surgeons undoubtedly bore similar witness to the value of the services of bandsmen in combat as well as their assistance in maintaining morale in camp.

On September 16, 1864, General W. B. Hazen wrote that during the Georgia campaign, and especially at Resaca, the removal of wounded from the firing line was much more promptly and efficiently performed by musicians than the "ambulance corps." The General said that was due to the good training of the musicians as stretcher bearers and also, to the low morale of infantry men who, detailed to the "ambulance corps," would have preferred serving with their units.

On very rare occasions bands rendered music to the wounded while still in the combat zone. After Antietam such an occasion actually occurred. A division hospital had been established to care for the wounded of a division which included casualties from "Hawkins' Zouaves" (9th New York Infantry). The wounded men had little to interest them in their recuperation until the band of the 9th by order of the regimental commander, marched from camp to play for the sick and wounded. The band gave its best selections, including "marching tunes," and, in addition, devoted several hours to playing and visiting from bed to bed, or, more correctly, from man to man, since there were no beds; the men slept on the ground.

14. Federal Band Music

The soldier, when at leisure, turned instinctively to his song. This could be patriotic, sentimental, and lighter music—a few of which have failed to survive because no censors would ever have passed them! The drum corps was limited entirely to martial music, but the band, with every available voice in the regiment, formed an orchestra and chorus for producing many types of songs.

In addition to instrumental performances by the bands, vocal music in the army was well-nigh universal. In quality it ranged from the extremely crude to the professional level. In many regiments there were glee clubs which formed the focal point of a general effort to improve the talent of the command. More frequently, single amateur musicians, without concerted endeavor, developed the musical ability of their own companies; the various companies uniting in a grand chorus when the entire regiment was stirred by a common impulse.

Vocal music became a part of the soldier's life as soon as the various company detachments were assembled in the State rendezvous areas, and the men became somewhat acquainted with each other and their surroundings. A soldier of the 14th New Hampshire Infantry tells us, that while in their long barracks at the State assembly camp, the men were just beginning to think of home and in such a mood, it was most natural that the men sing together. Perfectly in keeping with the occasion yet rather inappropriate as it is recalled, was the Southern melody which first trembled, then swelled through the barracks of a Union regiment when it was girding itself for the sanguinary strife:

It seemed indescribably sweet to our boyish imagination, as we lay there in the bottom bunk, on its fresh government-blanket with the big "U.S." in the middle wondering if the two-hundred-pound recruit above was likely to fall through and crush us; thinking also of the supper table at home, and a plate that was not turned and might never be again; when the plaintive sweet strain of the plantation song stole along from a single voice at the farther end of the barracks, caught up and augmented in volume as it rolled along, whose refrain was— "Alabama again! Alabama again! I'm going to go back to Alabama again."

In both armies, patriotic, sentimental, and comic songs mingled in considerable degree, but the lighter and more mirth-provoking songs were not too generally sung, while the questionable songs which might be expected to gain a prominent place in the freedom of unrestrained camp life were actually quite rare. Most of the soldiers on both sides were the products of semi-

Union forces pursuing Confederates through Mechanicsville, May 24, 1862. (Alfred R. Waud, May 1862. From the Library of Congress)

puritanical religious upbringing and it is exceedingly doubtful whether Americans ever fought in any other war in which religion played so important a role.

Especially popular were the better plantation melodies and the "war songs" of both sides. Unquestionably one of the greatest marching songs of all time is Julia Ward Howe's "Battle Hymn of the Republic." Also popular with Northern troops was "John Brown's Body," with an almost infinite variation in the verses.

Among the Confederate camp songs, the most popular were probably "Dixie" and "Maryland, My Maryland." There were many others sung by Southern units, ranging all the way from high merit to doggerel.

Often, it appears that rhythm was all-important. For example, here is a specimen of the rhythmic measures designed to fire the Southern heart:

The South, what though, despotic Abe
Now strive her power to kill,
Forever may her banner wave
And drive him at her will.

One of the Southern songs glorified their success in capturing Yankee merchant shipping. It went as follows:

And when our bloody work is done,
We sit us down at set of sun,
And then recount what glorious fun

213

Union forces lined up for inspection. The white gloves and clean uniforms always the subject of derisive comments from field soldiers. (From the Library of Congress)

It was to see the Yankees run
And strike their flag e'er the fight begun.

Just where the blood flowed in the above circumstances, it is difficult to imagine.

There was an indefinable charm in Negro melodies and they were listened to always with delight. The following is the first verse of a favorite with many Federal units:

In the Louisiana Lowlands, not many years ago,
There lived a colored gentleman, his name
was Pompey Snow

He played upon the banjo and on the tambourine
And, for rattling of the bones, Oh!
his like was never seen

In the Louisians Lowlands, Lowlands,
Lowlands,
In the Louisiana Lowlands, Low

The songs of the Federal soldier reflected his moods. These were often rollicking as, for example, when the men broke out with "When Johnny Comes Marching Home Again," or tender and plaintive as suggested in "We're Tenting Tonight On The Old Camp Ground," a song which was very popular in 1864 and 1865. The frightful losses at Andersonville and other Confederate prison pens gave special meaning to:

So within the prison cell
  We are waiting for the day

That shall come to open wide the iron door;
  And the hollow eye grows bright
And the poor heart almost gay
  As we think of seeing home and friends
    once more.

There were two other songs which expressed the deep sentiment, the enthusiasm, and the

Fife, drums, violin and a string bass, what an odd combination of instruments. (From the Library of Congress)

Regimental band of the 26th North Carolina. (From the Moravian Foundation) One of the more famous bands that served throughout the war, from Salem, North Carolina.

A colored band and a white bandmaster, band of the One Hundred Seventh U.S. Colored Infantry, probably around Washington, D.C. (A Brady photo from the Library of Congress)

unswerving purpose of the Federal volunteers, beyond all others sung around the camp fire. One was the culminating music of the war—planned by Grant and executed by Sherman:

Bring the good old bugle, boys!
We'll sing another song—
    Sing it with a spirit that will start the world along—
Sing it as we used to sing it, fifty thousand strong,
    While we were marching through Georgia.

The other song, on one occasion sung by the entire 19th Army Corps in the Shenandoah Valley, 1864, was always popular, both at the front and at home:

Yes, we'll rally round the flag, boys, rally once again,
Shouting the battle-cry of freedom'
    We will rally from the hillside,
We'll rally from the plain,
    Shouting the battle-cry of freedom!

On January 12, 1861, "Yankee Doodle" was hissed by Southern students who were present at the Academy of Music in Philadelphia. Again, at the surrender of Fort Sumter, a band played "Yankee Doodle" and "Hail Columbia" as the garrison left the fort on their return to New York.

In 1861, while Colonel Fletcher Webster's 12th Massachusetts Infantry was encamped at Fort Warren, Boston Harbor, the regiment included the Brockton Military Band. The Brockton Band adopted "Glory Hallelujah" as a song, and, when superseded by Patrick Gilmore and his band, the latter took it up and played it on all occasions. Gilmore later published the march. With Gilmore and his band in the lead, the 12th Massachusetts marched down Broadway in New York City, with everyone of its 1,000 men singing the new song. They sang it through Philadelphia and the length of Pennsylvania

Avenue in Washington. Soon its echo was heard wherever Union Citizens gathered or soldiers grouped around campfires.

Many regiments, like the 3rd Michigan Infantry, marched through large cities on their way to Washington, playing "Dixie." This air was not recognized as Southern property until some time after the war broke out. Daniel D. Emmet from Ohio composed this for a walk around in minstrel shows and first sang this song in 1859 in New York.

While crossing over the Potomac into Virginia, the band of the 79th New York "Highlanders" struck up the very appropriate air, "All the Blue Bonnets are Over the Border." The regiment passed the camp of the 69th New York; and as they approached the band played "The Campbells are coming."

Two days after the Federal defeat at First Bull Run, the 12th Massachusetts Infantry, 1,040 strong, marched through Boston on its way to the front. Its band played "John Brown's Body," a song which had been enthusiastically adopted by the 12th and which was soon to be set to the more inspiring words of Julia Ward Howe. On arrival in New York City the band again struck up "John Brown's Body"; the men joined in the singing, and the citizens of New York "were electrified." The song had never before been sung in New York. After arrival in Washington, the great marching tune was again played. One afternoon Julia Ward Howe heard it as marching troops sang it in going past. She, regretting that such a magnificent air had such poor words, wrote the famous lines as we know them today—a mighty, thrilling battle march which has thrilled listeners, here and abroad, for a hundred years.

The 9th New York Heavy Artillery, stationed for a long time in the defenses of Washington, had a large band. Although eventually it could play a large range of selections, its initial repertoire was extremely limited. The band concentrated on mastering "Belle Brandon," a favorite of the time, but one of the field officers wearied of this piece. One day, at dress parade, he sent word to the band that this air, although beautiful, had been played too much, and would the band play something else for a change!

The nucleus of the band was the old Rose Brass Band of civilian days; several ex-members of that organization were enlisted in the 9th Band.

On one occasion, the band was called on to play at a military funeral. Everything went according to schedule until the funeral procession was ready to start. But then, when the band leader was to give the signal for a selection appropriate to the occasion, he "found his wits wandering" and could not, for his life, think of a single marching piece that would be sufficiently sad. Nothing better than the long meter Doxology occurred to him, so he gave word, and "his boys pumped away on the familiar notes." In vain did the surgeon accompanying the funeral procession try to get his horse in step. Finally, he turned to the perspiring band leader and said: "What kind of a tune do you call that? I thought I could march to almost anything, but I'll be blamed if I can get this horse into step with Old Hundred." Just then the band leader's wits came back to him, and with an imperious wave of his hand, he switched the boys off into the "Dead March in Saul," and to the strains of "Unveil thy bosom, faithful tomb" the body was borne to its burial.

One of the favorite songs to which an additional verse was added for each year of the war ran as follows:

> In Eighteen Hundred and Sixty-One
> Free-ball! Free-ball!
> In Eighteen Hundred and Sixty-one
> Free-ball! Free-ball!

> In Eighteen Hundred and Sixty-one
> The War had then but just begun
> And we'll all drink stone blind
> Johnny, fill up the bowl

The latter verse brought many a smile to veterans because it involuntarily brought to mind the text of some of the other verses "which would hardly look well in print."

A favorite piece with the Army of the Potomac was "Hell on the Rappahannock." This lively number was performed with blaring brasses and much flourishing of drumsticks.

Some regiments had their own music composed for them. While the 4th Massachusetts Battalion was at Fort Independence, the famous Patrick S. Gilmore contributed his "Fourth Battalion Quickstep," the delightful strains of which were to accompany the men on many a march. The 4th later was merged with the 24th Massachusetts Infantry, whose band was under the leadership of Gilmore.

It was Gilmore also, who, while stationed in New Orleans, composed the popular "When Johnny Comes Marching Home Again," the words of which he wrote under the *nom de plume* of Louis Lambert.

A favorite song of the 11th New York Cavalry went as follows:

> I heard the bugle sound the calls for reveille and
> drill, for water, stable, and tattoo, for
> taps and all was still
> I heard it sound the sick call grim, and see the
> men in line,
> With faces awry as they drink their whiskey
> and quinine.
> Oh, did you see us in the street
> Dressed up in army blue,
> When drums and trumpets into town
> Our storm of music threw?

In September 1861 the 22nd New York employed F. B. Helmsmuller to head a band of 44 pieces. He was an excellent musician

The inauguration of Lincoln. March 1861.

and soon the band became famous. Helmsmuller composed a march which he dedicated to the 22nd and which was based, according to some critics, on a celebrated Austrian march. Be that as it may, this march was *the* regimental march for many years and "its swinging rhythm will never be forgotten by the officers and men who so often marched to its strains." The 22nd took its band to the front in 1862. In Baltimore it attracted a great deal of attention. But it was a very expensive luxury and was sent home in July 1862. The 13th Massachusetts Infantry had a band which often played from the "opera of Grenada" at dress parade. To this air the boys fitted the following words: "Corporal of the guard, corporal of the guard, Corporal of the guard, post eight." This tune remained popular with the 13th throughout its entire service. It was frequently played by the band of the 13th, but after the discharge of the band, early in September 1862, it was heard no more.

Regimental histories contain frequent reference to the popular "Bully for You." The historian of the 63rd Pennsylvania Infantry thought so much of this air that he reproduced the sheet music in the regiment's history. He also included "The Bully Old Sixty-Third," composed by a member of the regiment.

Men of the 27th Massachusetts Infantry, regretted the loss of their band. The morale of the band had always been high, and the soldiers missed the band's rendition of "Lee's March," "Kate Kearney," and "Widow Machree." An original piece by a member of the band, "Lee's March," was named in honor of the colonel of the regiment, Horace C. Lee.

Lincoln was fond of music and military bands. Although he liked to listen to the many regimental bands of 1861-1862, he especially liked the concerts of the Marine Bands. Interestingly enough, Lincoln liked "Dixie" and asked that it be played when news was received of Lee's surrender.

Although General Lee greatly admired band music, his adversary, General Grant, had no use for such music; in fact, Grant had no ear at all for music or rhythm and never kept step to the band music, no matter how vigorously the bass drums emphasized the beat. When walking in company with others, the General made no attempt to keep in step. On one occasion, shortly after the Wilderness, a drum corps in passing caught sight of the General and at once struck up a then popular Negro camp-meeting air. Everyone present began to laugh, and Grant's aide, Rawlins, cried out: "Good for the drummers!" "What's the fun?" asked Grant. "Why," Rawlins replied, "Why they are playing 'Ain't I glad to get out of de Wilderness.'" Grant smiled at the wit of the musicians, and said, "Well, with me a musical joke always requires explanation. I know only two tunes—one is 'Yankee Doodle,' and the other isn't."

Later that summer, at City Point an unsuspecting commander sent a band over to Grant's headquarters to play during the dinner hour. After two such periods of dinner music, the General, sitting at the mess table, remarked: "I've noticed that that band always begins its noise just about the time I am sitting down to dinner and want to talk." An aide took the hint and went over to the band. The bandsmen, gorgeously uniformed, were equipped with "every sort of brass instrument ever invented, from a diminutive cornet with pistons to a gigantic double-bass horn." The band master was puffing with all the vigor of a quack-medicine advertisement, his eyes riveted upon the music, and the aide had considerable difficulty in getting the worthy's attention. Eventually he succeeded, and the band master "with a look of disinheritance on his countenance" sadly marched his band back

"Thirteenth Wisconsin band." Thirteenth regiment band, Wisconsin Volunteer Infantry directed by L.W. Eastman. Photos made in 1865 in Huntsville, Alabama.

to camp. On the aide's return, Grant said, "I fear that band-master's feelings have been hurt, but I didn't want him to be wasting his time upon a person who has no ear for music." A staff officer remarked: "Well, General, you were at least more considerate than Commodore———, who, the day he came to take command of his vessel, and was seated at dinner in the cabin, heard music on deck, and immediately sent for the executive officer and said to him: "Have the instruments *and men* of that band thrown overboard at once!"

At Meade's headquarters no "clap-trap" music was permitted. The band of the 114th Pennsylvania Infantry (Collis' Zouaves) was only permitted to play the "choicest pieces." It did not take long to learn the style of music which pleased Meade—any "pretty flowing melody, smoothly arranged, whether operatic or ballad, had a great charm for him." When Meade was not familiar with any selection played for him, he would send his orderly to learn the names of the piece and composer.

Religious music was much in vogue in the later years of the war. In the area of the 114th Pennsylvania, a neat chapel was erected and prominent clergymen visited the army to give sermons. General Seth Williams of the Army of the Potomac had charge of these "parish arrangements" and requested the band of the 114th to prepare suitable pieces for the services. The band master of the 114th suggested "Der Dag des Hern" (The Day of Our Lord) or "Die Kapelle" (The Chapel). But General Williams was concerned over the lack of available singing talent. The band offered to supply an impromptu quartet. The General, much pleased, sent to Washington for hymn books, and even suggested getting a cabinet organ. This instrument, however, was too heavy to be transported. Nevertheless, the religious services were a success; generals,

cabinet officers, and eminent clergymen were in attendance, including Bishop Whipple of Minnesota, whose Episcopal vestments and sermon impressed all his listeners.

Not all instrumental music in the army was enlivening. Tenderly mournful were the burial dirges of band or drum corps, coming with a frequency which established a dreadful monotony of death, the file of soldiers marching slowly, with arms reversed; the tune being usually that most beautiful and simple of death marches "Pleyel's Hymn." Every softened note of the fife, every throb of the muffled drum, tore tender cords in the hearts of surviving comrades. Some of the mourners were themselves soon to prolong the sad procession, with no members of their family to be present at the final rites.

Both North and South had many publishers who turned out songbooks for sale to the soldiers. Pocket songbooks were very popular both with the soldiers and also back home. Although Beadle songbooks were probably the most numerous, there were many others of varying popularity.

It is very difficult to list even a fraction of the songs which were popular with the soldiers. This popularity varied from state to state and camp to camp. The following list is an attempt to indicate those which unquestionably enjoyed popularity in the camps.

Some of the most popular songs of the War:

FEDERAL

The Battle-Cry of Freedom—George F. Root
Three Hundred Thousand More—
  James Gibbons
Battle Hymn of the Republic—
  Julia Ward Howe
John Brown's Body—Thomas B. Bishop
Weeping, Sad and Lonely—Charles C. Sawyer
Hard Crackers, Come Again No More—
When Johnny Comes Marching Home—
  Thomas B. Bishop

Grafted Into the Army—Henry Clay Work
Tramp, Tramp, Tramp—George F. Root
Yankee Doodle—
The Star Spangled Banner—
The Girl I Left Behind Me—
Johnny Fill Up the Bowl—
Home Sweet Home—
Annie Laurie—
Old Hundred—
Pop Goes the Weasel—
Come Where My Love Lies Dreaming—
Who will Care for Mother Now—
    Charles C. Sawyer

There was an amazingly large number of songs about drummer boys. The following is a partial list:

The Drummer Boy of Antietam—words and
    music by Albert Fleming
Drummer Boy of Vicksburg—words and music
    by P. DeGeer
The Dying Drummer Boy—words by J. C. Koch,
    music by L. Grube
The Dying Drummer—words by Thomas
    Manahan, music by Mrs. Parkhurst
The Dying Drummer Boy—words by Mary
    Lathbury, music by E. C. Howe
The Drummer Boy of Shiloh—words and music
    by Will Hays

15. Confederate Band Music

Confederates generally tended to stick to old favorites which they had grown to love before they went away to war. Among the most popular of these were "Home Sweet Home", "Annie Laurie", "Listen to the Mocking Bird", "Juanita", "Lorena", and "The Girl I Left Behind Me."

The following is a list of some of the most popular Confederate songs:

"The Cavaliers of Dixie"—Benjamin F. Porter
"Dixie"—Daniel Decatur Emmett
"The Bonnie Blue Flag"—Harry Macarthy
"Lorena"—H. D. L. Webster
"Maryland, My Maryland"—
    James Ryder Randall
"Eating Goober Peas"—A. Pender
"Oh, I'm a Good Old Rebel"—
"The Southern Soldier Boy"—G. W. Alexander

"Dixie" with its spirited tempo was adopted by the South and this minstrel air, composed by a Northerner, soon became the Confederacy's national air. In 1861 Confederate bands everywhere played "Dixie," although many other songs soon appeared. The many military organizations in the Southern states had marches and polkas written in their honor, while the great leaders of the new country had individual songs written in their honor. Such prominent figures as Jefferson Davis, Jackson, Beauregard, and Lee, each had several pieces of music composed expressly for them, while the number of lesser officers so honored was substantial.

Confederate bands played the airs which they knew from childhood; these included, of course, those of national popularity which had become a part of the Republic's musical heritage. Thus, when Jubal Early's troops moved into a Pennsylvania town, the Confederates marched to the tune of "Yankee Doodle." However, this kindly gesture to Antebellum days did not deter "Old Applejack" from levying a requisition of $28,000.00 on the town—in Yankee money! He burned the town when the money was not forthcoming.

When the Confederates marched out to surrender at Appomattox there were no Confederate bands to escort the flags and to pace the marching columns. In their hectic retreating and their fighting of delaying actions, the Confederates had lost most of their instruments. The only bands heard were those of the Federals, but these were kept away from the surrender area as a token of consideration for the feelings of the vanquished enemy. The Federal band music was heard from a distance only.

On October 13, 1863, Quantrill reported that he came upon a camp some 45 miles south of Fort Scott, Kansas, drove the Federals for 4 miles, and in the Federal camp captured a "fine brass band and wagon, fully rigged."

As the Federals' aggressive lines pushed up Missionary Ridge, Confederate centers of resistance continued to hold out as long as possible. Groups of riflemen stood their ground and fought back. Among them were elements of the 20th Tennessee Infantry whose colonel ordered the band to strike up "Dixie." This rallied the regiment as nothing else could have done.

The Confederates had very little organized amusement for themselves and music—in some form or other—was very probably their favorite recreation. They were especially fond of such sentimental songs as "Lorena"; "Faded Flowers"; "Who Will Care for Mother Now"; and "Home Sweet Home."

One of the popular Southern productions was John R. Thompson's "Music in Camp." The setting was immediately after the battle of Chancellorsville and stressed the exchanges between the soldiers in lulls of active campaigning. Three of the stanzas are especially appropriate:

A Federal band, which, eve and morn,
    Played measures brave and nimble,
Had just struck up, with flute and horn
    And lively clash of cymbal.

Down flocked the soldiers to the banks,
    Til, margined with its pebbles,
One wooded shore was blue with "Yanks"
    And one was gray with "Rebels".

Then all was still
    and then the band
With movement light and tricksy
Made stream and forest,
    hill and strand,
Reverberate with "Dixie."

"Maryland, My Maryland," composed by James R. Randall, was set to the music of the German song "O Tannenbaum." James Russell Lowell deemed Randall's words to be the finest poem inspired by the war. In April 1861, Randall, a native of Maryland, but residing at the time in Louisiana, composed this poem to inspire Maryland—to join the Confederacy.

16. Bugle Calls

Most of the bugle calls were borrowed from European armies and had centuries of tradition behind them. The bugle calls of the Civil War differ widely from those used in recent decades. This is due primarily to the adoption of General Emory Upton's new drill system in 1867, wherein there was much standardization accomplished with the many varied calls of the 1860's. Although the origins of many calls are obscure, the following information is of interest in showing the antiquity of some of the more common calls of the war:

"Retreat" was originally a French cavalry call and reportedly goes back to the Crusades. By "Retreat" is meant the ceremony at sunset and not retreat from the enemy.

"Tattoo" can be traced back to the Thirty Years War (1618–1648).

"Boots and Saddles" is reportedly of English origin. The same call in the French cavalry is in exactly the same rhythm as ours, but begins a fifth lower. Ours, therefore, would seem to be derived from the French.

The hunting horn quality of the bugle carried its tone for long distances. There were bugle calls for reveille, breakfast, sick call, dinner, supper, for sergeants, adjutant reports, report of officers to the colonel, "fall in" for companies, roll call, guard mount, plus various calls for company and battalion drill. However, the use of the bugle in the various evolutions of the company or regiment in drill or combat was mostly confined to the cavalry and artillery.

It was at one time supposed that bugle calls could be used successfully in directing the skirmishing lines. Several units were drilled in responding to these bugle calls, but it was discovered that the majority of men never did learn to distinguish the different calls. In fact, some observers believed that the bugle calls only served to warn the enemy of the forthcoming movements.

A comprehensive treatment of the various calls of the Civil War would fill a large and entertaining volume by itself. The bugle call at reveille, on the skirmish line, or guiding the evolutions of squadron or battery, continued to echo in veterans' ears long after the war was over. The airs of fife and horn lingered for years about farms, shops, stores, and offices; welcome reminiscences of tunes and experiences which the men never forgot.

The "calls" were important and perpetual! While the worn-out soldier would question any pleasant association with the tantalizing drum sounding the call for another detail to appear in front of the adjutant's quarters, nevertheless, much of the genuine romance of camp life was associated with the routine "calls." There was no finer inspiration thrilling the entire nervous system of a vigorous soldier than the first burst, crash, and roll of reveille when a crack drum corps with melodious shrill fife rallied upon the color line and roused an entire regiment as by an electric shock. On a bright morning or in the middle of a driving rainstorm, nothing ushered in the day as did reveille in a military camp. The effect was intensified when, in a great Army stretching out for miles, a single bugle note gave the signal, and then, as by magic, from every direction broke out and rolled on in one mass of accelerating sound the roll of drums, the screech of fifes, and the blare of artillery and cavalry bugles.

The breakfast call thirty minutes later was mainly suggestive of slab bacon and was accompanied by the rattle of tin plates, quart cups, and iron spoons. Then at 8:30 A.M. came the sick call; and the mournful, ludicrous procession gathered from each company converged at the surgeon's quarters. There was seen the faithful soldier who had fought off disease, and stood at his post until at last, in a ruined physique, had qiute succumbed. And in the procession were always to be found the chronic "deadbeats"; they deliberately cheated their government and cause. These men were lazy scamps and arrant cowards, and they shifted every burden of duty on to their overworked comrades. Rheumatism was the favorite dodge; and the victims became not too helpless, but just helpless enough. The surgeons well knew they were shamming, but it was difficult to demonstrate the fact; and finally a discharge was granted, simply to abate a nuisance. There was a great deal of peculiar music in the surgeon's call.

There followed calls for guard mounting and dinner. The historian of the 14th New Hampshire Infantry told how he and his comrades recalled the pleasant face of their favorite old drummer, Sanborn, beating the long roll as no one else could beat it, his arms playing all about him like forked lightning, his drum sticks rattling down upon the drum head like half a dozen magnificent hailstorms, each combination of sounds welling up and flying off like distant peals of thunder with no room for reverberation between the claps. "That genial old drummer, gone to his rest, never dreamed of the stir he made in the bosoms of his comrades. His dinner-call is sounding still."

Every call, march, and air of band and drum corps entered into the very life of a regiment, and was valued beyond the power of a civilian to appreciate. The evening calls of supper, tattoo, and taps were full of music and meaning, and each breathed forth its own suggestions. At tattoo a military camp was an interesting study; games, letter-writing, reading, mending, lounging on bunks, story-telling, these were intruded upon by the drum major in his preliminary flourish, leading to taps. If the sergeant of the guard, who checked down each company street, could have gathered up the comments occasionally hurled after him, he could have presented posterity with an extremely interesting but unprintable collection of American colloquialisms.

The acme of military music was reached at the dress parade, and it was never determined whether a crack drum corps or a fine band appeared to best advantage on these occasions. For martial music, purely, a drum corps was considered to be unrivaled; while a band possessed obvious advantages and constantly served to promote morale. One thing was certain; no regiment with a band maintained a first rate drum corps. This could not be expected of any command in active service. The 14th New Hampshire Infantry was one of the few regiments in the Federal army which, through all the vicissitudes of an arduous campaign, through swift marches, rapid retreats, and great battles, still maintained a good band to play the jaunty column into its day's march, and the wearied files into the welcome camp at night.

When an army started out, the buglers sounded "the general," which was a call to alert each brigade to be prepared to move. Shortly thereafter, the buglers sounded "assembly" and the companies formed in line in their company streets. Then the buglers sounded "to the color" and the regimental color bearers took the covers off their battle flags. In turn, regiment after regiment moved out on the highway, bands playing, with great rolling of drums and unforgettable pageantry.

Calls varied with regiments and with the three branches of service—Infantry, Cavalry, and Artillery.

Up to July 1862, the infantry call for "Taps" was that set down in Casey's *Tactics*, probably borrowed from the French. But soon after the Army of the Potomac had retired to Harrison's Landing (after the "Seven Days" battles), General Dan Butterfield composed his version of "Taps," and had the headquarters bugler play it in lieu of Casey's "regulation" version. Soon the buglers from other units picked it up until Butterfield's composition came into general use in the Army of the Potomac. Reportedly, it was then taken to the Western armies by the 11th and 12th Corps when they were transferred to Chattanooga in the fall of 1863. Years after the war, a veteran remarked that he could still hear the echo of the bugle calls for "Reveille," and "Retreat," and "Dan, Dan, Dan Butterfield, Butterfield," as they had sounded back in 1861. This veteran assured General Butterfield that the echoes "will linger forever in the brain and heart of every survivor of the old Brigade."

In the 1st Connecticut Heavy Artillery "Tattoo" was at 10 P.M. at which time the men fell in for roll call. At 10:30 P.M. three taps of the drum was the signal for extinguishing all lights and for all noise to cease.

In the mounted regiments—artillery and cavalry—the army day began with the first bugle call, known to the artilleryman as the "Assembly of Buglers," to which the sergeant or corporal of the guard would call up the bugler; "Assembly of Buglers" was sounded in summer at about 5 A.M. and in winter at 6 A.M. This call routed the men out of their tents. In 15 minutes the next call, "Assembly" at which the men lined up in the company street—called to attention and dressed by the first sergeant—and then, while at "Parade Rest" listened to "Reveille" played by the buglers. Then followed "Roll Call" and the day's activities began.

In cavalry and artillery units, the day's work began with "Stable Call" at which time the men cleaned their mounts and put nosebags on them. Following close upon the completion of their stable routine, the men were called to mess by "Breakfast Call." Generally, at 8 A.M. "Sick Call" was sounded, followed (in mounted units) by "Water Call," and then "Fatigue Call," and then "Drill Call." If the drill was for mounted men, the call was "Boots and Saddles." At noon "Dinner Call" brought the men to eat. The next regular call for the mounted units was "Water Call" (4 P.M.). On the return of the horses, "Stable Call" was again sounded. At about 5:45 P.M., "Attention" was sounded, soon to be followed by "Assembly" when the men fell in again for their "Retreat" roll-call. "Retreat" in the mounted units corresponded with "Dress Parade" for the infantry.

In some artillery units (and maybe others as well) the bugle again sounded "Attention" at 8:30 P.M., followed by the "Assembly" about 8:35 P.M., whereupon the men fell in for their final roll-call, known as "Tattoo."

The "Tattoo" of the artillery was the "Taps" of the infantry; the calls themselves were identical. At the conclusion of the call, a drummer beat a few single isolated taps which closed out the army day. At this signal all lights were supposed to be put out, all talking and other noises ceased and every soldier, except the guard, was in his quarters.

It was not long before the recruit cavalrymen learned that their horses also learned both the drill and the various bugle calls. This was equally true for the artillery units whose horses soon responded promptly to the bugle calls of "March," "Wheel," and "Halt." As the writer can testify from personal experience, well-trained horses respond even more quickly to bugle calls than do their riders.

Although buglers, as a class, were much maligned because they always seemed to be waking men up or calling them to unpleasant drill or fatigue duty, apparently a few of these individuals achieved "honor in their time." For example, on October 15, 1863, Bugler Edward F. Chard, Co. "C" 1st Massachusetts Heavy Artillery, was presented with a bugle by the commissioned officers of his regiment as a token of respect and appreciation for his "good conduct and attention to duty." There were other similar cases during the war.

Infantry tactics by BVT. Major General Emory Upton, United States Army, 1867. Revised in 1880.

Trumpet signals or bugle signals. In large camps or garrisons, marches are played in the streets, or in front of the quarters between the "Assembly of Trumpeters" and "Reveille" and "Tattoo."

The memorizing of these signals will be facilitated by observing that all movements to the right are on the ascending chord, that corresponding movements to the left are on the descending chord; and that the changes of gait are all upon the same note.

There are sixty-seven trumpet or bugle calls of which we show thirteen:

1. Assembly of trumpeters
2. Assembly
3. Reveille
4. Retreat
5. Tattoo
6. Extinguish lights
7. Mess
8. Sick
9. School
10. Church
11. Drill
12. To the Colors
13. Pack up

Bibliography

PRIMARY SOURCES

War of the Rebellion: A Compilation of the Official Records of the Union and Confederate Armies, 128 serial volumes and 3 volumes of atlases. Washington, 1880-1901.

General Orders, U. S. War Department, Adjutant General's Office, 1861-1865.

General Orders, C. S. War Department, Adjutant General's Office, 1861-1865.

Revised Regulations for the Army of the United States 1861, editions of 1861 and 1863, Washington, 1861, 1863.

Army Regulations Adopted for the Use of the Confederate States, Editions of 1861 and 1863, Richmond, 1861, 1863.

United States National Archives. Much manuscript material on bands and bandsmen of the 1861-1865 period.

Manuscript letters of Musician Roland F. Barrows, Regimental Band, 18th Massachusetts Infantry.

SECONDARY SOURCES

Abbott, John S. C., *The History of the Civil War in America,* 2 vols., New York 1863, 1866.

Abbott, Stephen G., *The First Regiment New Hampshire Volunteers . . .* Keene, N. H., 1890.

Albert, Allen D., *History of the Forty-Fifth Regiment,* Williamsport, Pa., 1912.

Ambrose, D. Leib, *History of the Seventh Regiment Illinois Volunteer Infantry,* Springfield, Ill., 1868.

Anonymous, *Record of the Service of the Forty-Fourth Massachusetts, Boston,* 1887.

———, *Ninety-Second Illinois Volunteers,* Freeport, 1875.

———, *Society of the Seventy-Fourth Illinois Volunteer Infantry,* Rockford, Ill., 1903.

———, *Personal Reminiscences and Experiences,* (103rd Ohio Infantry), Oberlin, N. D.

Bardeen, C. W., *A Little Fifer's War Diary,* Syracuse, N. Y., 1910.

Bates, Samuel P., *History of Pennsylvania Volunteers,* 5 vols., Harrisburg, 1869.

Baylor, George, *Bull Run to Bull Run: or, Four Years in the Army of Northern Virginia,* Richmond, 1900.

Benedict, George Grenville, *Army Life in Virginia,* Burlington, Vt., 1895.

Bennett, Edwin C., *Musket and Sword,* Boston, 1900.

Billings, John D., *Hardtack and Coffee,* Boston, 1889.

Bishop, J. W., *The Story of a Regiment: Second Regiment of Minnesota Veteran Volunteer Infantry,* St. Paul, Minn., 1890.

Botkin, B. A., *A Civil War Treasury of Tales, Legends and Folklore*, New York, 1960.

Brown, Henri Le Febre, *History of the Third Regiment Excelsior Brigade (72nd New York Infantry)*, Jamestown, N. Y., 1902.

Browne, Richard Wentworth, "Memoranda on the Civil War," *The Century Magazine*, Vol. XXXV, January, 1888.

Bruce, George A., *The Twentieth Regiment of Massachusetts Volunteer Infantry*, Boston, 1906.

Buffum, Francis H., *A Memorial of the Great Rebellion . . . Fourteenth Regiment New Hampshire Volunteers*, Boston, 1882.

Butterfield, Daniel, *Camp and Outpost Duty for Infantry*, New York, 1863.

Butterfield, Julia Lorrilard, *A Biolgraphical Memorial of General Daniel Butterfield*, New York, 1904.

Caldwell, J. F. J., *The History of a Brigade of South Carolinians Known First as "Gregg's" and Subsequently as "McGowan's" Brigade*, Philadelphia, 1866.

Carter, W. R., *History of the First Regiment of Tennessee Volunteer Cavalry*, Knoxville, 1902.

Casler, John O., *Four Years in the Stonewall Brigade*, Guthrie, Oklahoma, 1893.

Chamberlin, Thomas, *History of the 150th Pennsylvania Volunteers*, Philadelphia, 1905.

Clark, Emmons, *History of the Seventh Regiment of New York 1809-1889*, 2 vols., New York, 1890.

Clark, Walter (editor), *Histories of the Several Regiments and Battalions from North Carolina in the Great War 1861-1865*, 5 vols., Raleigh and Goldsboro, 1901.

Cogswell, Leander W., *A History of the Eleventh New Hampshire . . . Infantry*, Concord, 1891.

Confederate Veteran, 1892-1932.

Cooke, John Esten, *Wearing of the Gray*, New York, 1867.

Crowell, Joseph E., *The Young Volunteer*, New York, 1906.

Crowingshield, B. W., *A History of the First Regiment . . . Massachusetts Cavalry*, Boston, 1891.

Davis, Burke, *Our Incredible Civil War*, New York, 1960.

Davis, Charles E., Jr., *Three Years in the Army*, Boston, 1894.

Davis, W. W. H., *History of the 104th Pennsylvania Regiment*, Philadelphia, 1866.

Dawes, Rufus R., *Service with the Sixth Wisconsin Volunteers*, Marietta, Ohio, 1890.

DeTrobriand, Regis, *Four Years with the Army of the Potomac*, Boston, 1889.

Denny, J. Waldo, *Wearing the Blue*, Worcester, 1879.

Derby, W. P., *Bearing Arms in the Twenty-Seventh Massachusetts Regiment*, Boston, 1883.

Emilio, Luis F., *History of the Fifty-Fourth Regiment*, Boston, 1894.

Emmerton, James A., *A Record of the Twenty-Third Regiment Massachusetts Volunteer Infantry*, Boston, 1886.

Floyd, David Bittle, *History of the Seventy-Fifth . . . Indiana Infantry*, Philadelphia, 1893.

Freeman, Douglas Southall, *R. E. Lee*, 4 vols., New York, 1941.

Goldsborough, W. W., *The Maryland Line in the Confederate States Army*, Baltimore, 1869.

Gordon, John B., *Reminiscenes of the Civil War*, New York, 1903.

Hall, Harry H., *A Johnny Reb Band from Salem*, Raleigh, N. C., 1963.

Hanson, John W., *Historical Sketch of the Old Sixth Regiment*, Boston, 1866.

Harwell, Richard B., *Confederate Music*, Chapel Hill, N. C., 1950.

Hays, Gilbert Adams, *Under the Red Patch (63rd Pennsylvania Infantry)*, Pittsburgh, 1908.

Heaps, Willard A. and Porter W., *The Singing Sixties,* Norman, Oklahoma, 1960.

Houghton, Edwin B., *The Campaigns of the Seventeenth Maine,* Portland, 1866.

Kieffer, Harry M., *The Recollections of a Drummer Boy,* 6th Edition, Boston, 1889.

Kobbe, Gustav, "The Trumpet in Camp and Battle," *The Century Magazine,* Vol. LVI, No. 4, August, 1898.

LaBree, Ben. (Editor), *Camp Fires of the Confederacy,* Louisville, 1898.

Leech, Margaret, *Reveille in Washington,* New York, 1941.

Lockwood, James D., *Life and Adventures of a Drummer Boy,* Albany, N. Y., 1893.

Lord, Edward O., *History of the Ninth Regiment New Hampshire Volunteers,* Concord, 1895.

Lucke, Jerome B., *History of the New Haven Grays,* New Haven, 1876.

Mann, Albert W., *History of the Forty-Fifth Regiment,* N. P., 1908.

Mark, Penrose G., *Red, White, and Blue Badge (93rd Pennsylvania Infantry),* 1911.

Marvin, Edwin E., *The Fifth Regiment Connecticut Volunteers,* Hartford, 1889.

McClellan, H. B., *The Life and Campaigns of Major General J. E. B. Stuart,* Boston, 1885.

McKim, Randolph, *A Soldier's Recollections,* New York, 1910.

McMurray, W. J., *History of the Twentieth Tennessee Regiment Volunteer Infantry,* Nashville, 1904.

Miller, Francis T. (editor), *Photographic History of the Civil War,* 10 vols., New York, 1912.

Moore, Frank (editor), *Lyrics of Loyalty,* New York, 1864; *Personal and Political Ballards,* New York, 1864; *Songs of the Soldiers,* New York, 1864; *Rebel Rhymes and Rhapsodies,* New York, 1864.

Muffly, J. W., *The Story of Our Regiment (148th Pennsylvania Infantry),* Des Moines, 1904.

Owen, William M., *In Camp and Battle with the Washington Artillery,* Boston, 1885.

Page, Charles D., *History of the Fourteenth Regiment, Connecticut Volunteer Infantry,* Meriden, 1906.

Porter, Horace, *Campaigning with Grant,* New York, 1897.

Preston, N. D., *History of the Tenth Regiment (New York) Cavalry,* New York, 1892.

Prowell, George R., *History of York County, Pa.,* Vol. 1, Chicago, 1907; *History of the 87th Pennsylvania Volunteers,* York, 1903.

Pullen, John J., *The Twentieth Maine,* New York, 1957.

Rauscher, Frank, *Music on the March,* Philadelphia, 1892.

Reed, John A., *History of the 101st Regiment Pennsylvania . . . Infantry,* Chicago, 1910.

Rock, R. W., *History of the Eleventh Regiment, Rhode Island Volunteers,* Providence, 1881.

Roe, Alfred S., *The Ninth New York Heavy Artillery,* Worcester, Mass, 1899; *The Tenth Regiment Massachusetts Volunteer Infantry 1861-1864,* Springfield, Mass., 1909; *The Thirty-Ninth Regiment Massachusetts Volunteers 1862-1865,* Worcester, Mass., 1914.

Silber, Irwin, *Songs of the Civil War,* New York, 1960.

Small, Harold Adams (editor), *The Road to Richmond,* Berkeley, Calif., 1939.

Smith, Thomas West, *The Story of a Cavalry Regiment (11th New York Cavalry),* New York, 1897.

Spear, Ellis, "The Story of the Raising and Organization of a Regiment of Volunteers in 1862"; *War Paper* No. 46, D. C. Commandery, Loyal Legion of the United States, 1903.

Swinton, Williams, *History of the Seventh Regiment . . . (New York),* New York, 1870.

Taylor, Benj. F., *Pictures of Life in Camp*

and Field (3rd Edition), Chicago, 1884.

Taylor, Frank H., *Philadelphia in the Civil War*, Philadelphia, 1913.

Thomas, H. W., *History of the Doles-Cook Brigade of Northern Virginia*, Atlanta, 1903.

Thompson, S. Millett, *Thirteenth Regiment of New Hampshire Volunteer Infantry*, Boston, 1888.

Todd, William, *The Seventy-Ninth Highlanders New York Volunteers*, Albany, 1886.

Ulmer, George T., *Adventures and Reminiscences of a Volunteer or a Drummer Boy from Maine*, N. P., 1892.

Vail, Enos B., *Reminiscences of a Boy in the Civil War*, privately printed, 1915.

Vaill, Theodore F., *History of the Second Connecticut Volunteer Heavy Artillery*, Winsted, Conn., 1868.

Walker, William C., *History of the Eighteenth Regiment Connecticut Volunteers*, Norwich, 1885.

Ward, Joseph R. C., *History of the One Hundred and Sixth Regiment Pennsylvania Volunteers*, Philadelphia, 1883.

White, William Carter, *A History of Military Music in America*, New York, 1944.

Wiley, Bell Irvin, *The Life of Billy Yank*, Indianapolis, 1951; *The Life of Johnny Reb*, Indianapolis, 1943.

Wingate, George W., *History of the Twenty-Second Regiment (N.Y.N.G.)*, New York, 1896.

Discography

Songs of the North and South. Sung by Frank Luther and Zor Layman. New York, Decca Records, DL 8093.

The Confederacy. Richard Bales, National Gallery Orchestra, and Choir. New York, Columbia Records, DL 220.

The Union. Richard Bales, National Gallery Orchestra, and Choir. New York, Columbia Records, DL 244.

Ballads of the Civil War. Moses Asch. New York, Folkways Records, FH 5004.

Songs and Ballads of America's Wars. Sung by Frank Warner. New York, Elektra Records, EKL 13.

The Civil War. Frederick Fennell and the Eastman Wind Ensemble. Gerald C. Stowe, military adviser; Martin Gabel, narrator. Band and field music of the Union and Confederate armies, played on original Civil War instruments. Two volumes, Mercury Records.

Index